Bill Bright taught us to follow the example of our Lord and to live a life of giving.

From the Foreword by
<small>CHARLES STANLEY</small>

BILL BRIGHT'S
"THE JOY OF KNOWING GOD"
SERIES

the JOY of DYNAMIC GIVING

DR. BILL BRIGHT

The Bible Teacher's Teacher

COOK COMMUNICATIONS MINISTRIES
Colorado Springs, Colorado • Paris, Ontario
KINGSWAY COMMUNICATIONS LTD
Eastbourne, England

Victor® is an imprint of
Cook Communications Ministries,
Colorado Springs, CO 80918
Cook Communications, Paris, Ontario
Kingsway Communications, Eastbourne, England

THE JOY OF DYNAMIC GIVING
© 2005 by Bill Bright

First Printing, 2005
Printed in United States of America
1 2 3 4 5 6 7 8 9 10 Printing/Year 09 08 07 06 05

Cover Design: Brand Navigation, LLC

Unless otherwise indicated, all Scripture quotations are taken from the
Holy Bible, New Living Translation, copyright © 1996. Used by permission of Tyndale House Publishers, Inc., Wheaton, Illinois 60189. All
rights reserved. Other versions used include the New King James
Version® (NKJV). Copyright © 1982 by Thomas Nelson, Inc. Used by
permission. All rights reserved; Scripture marked NIV is taken from the
HOLY BIBLE, NEW INTERNATIONAL VERSION®. Copyright © 1973,
1978, 1984 International Bible Society. Used by permission of
Zondervan. All rights reserved; Scripture quotations marked NASB are
taken from the NEW AMERICAN STANDARD BIBLE®, Copyright ©
1960, 1962, 1963, 1968, 1971, 1972, 1973, 1975, 1977, 1995 by The
Lockman Foundation. Used by permission (www.Lockman.org); Verses
marked TLB are taken from The Living Bible, © 1971, Tyndale House
Publishers, Wheaton, IL 60189. Used by permission; Scripture quotations marked NLV are from the New Life Bible, copyright © 1969 by
Christian Literature International. Used by permission. All rights
reserved; and the King James Version (KJV) (Public Domain). Italics in
Scripture have been added by the author for emphasis.

Library of Congress Cataloging-in-Publication Data

Bright, Bill.
    The joy of dynamic giving : the key to guilt-free living / Bill Bright.
        p. cm. -- (The joy of knowing God ; bk. 9)
    ISBN 0-7814-4254-0 (pbk.)
    1. Christian giving. 2. Stewardship, Christian. I. Title.
    BV772.B73 2005
    248'.6--dc22

                                2004026885

Dedication

GLOBAL FOUNDING PARTNERS

The Bright Media Foundation continues the multifaceted ministries of Bill and Vonette Bright for generations yet unborn. God has touched and inspired the Brights through the ministries of writers through the centuries. Likewise, they wish to pass along God's message in Jesus Christ as they have experienced it, seeking to inspire, train, and transform lives, thereby helping to fulfill the Great Commission each year until our Lord returns.

Many generous friends have prayed and sacrificed to support the Bright Media Foundation's culturally relevant, creative works, in print and electronic forms. The following persons specifically have helped to establish the foundation. These special friends will always be known as Global Founding Partners *of the Bright Media Foundation.*

Bill and Christie Heavener and family

Stuart and Debra Sue Irby and family

Edward E. Haddock Jr., Edye Murphy-Haddock, and the Haddock family

Acknowledgments

It was my privilege to share fifty-four years, six months, and twenty days of married life with a man who loved Jesus passionately and served Him faithfully. Six months before his home going, Bill initiated what has become "The Joy of Knowing God" series. It was his desire to pass along to future generations the insights God had given him that they, too, could discover God's magnificence and live out the wonderful plan He has for their lives.

"The Joy of Knowing God" series is a collection of Bill Bright's top ten life-changing messages. Millions of people around the world have already benefited greatly from these spiritual truths and are now living the exciting Christian adventure that God desires for each of us.

On behalf of Bill, I want to thank the following team that helped research, compile, edit, and wordsmith the manuscripts and audio scripts in this series: Jim Bramlett, Rebecca Cotton, Eric Metaxas, Sheryl Moon, Cecil Price, Michael Richardson, Eric Stanford, and Rob Suggs.

I also want to thank Bill's longtime friends and Campus Crusade associates Bailey Marks and Ted Martin, who carefully reviewed the scripts and manuscripts for accuracy.

Bill was deeply grateful to Bob Angelotti and Don Stillman of Allegiant Marketing Group for their encouragement to produce this series and their ingenuity in facilitating distribution to so many.

A special thanks to Cook Communications and its team of dedicated professionals who partnered with Bright Media Foundation in this venture, as well as to Steve Laube, who brought us together.

Last but not least, I want to express my appreciation to Helmut Teichert, who worked faithfully and diligently in overseeing this team that Bill's vision would be realized, and to John Nill, CEO of Bright Media, who has helped me navigate the many challenges along this journey.

As a result of the hard work of so many, and especially our wonderful Lord's promise of His grace, I trust that multitudes worldwide will experience a greater joy by knowing God and His ways more fully.

With a grateful heart,
MRS. BILL BRIGHT (VONETTE)

Contents

Foreword

The total worldwide outreach of Campus Crusade for Christ has been astonishing. This has been made possible only because of God's giving nature: He gave His only begotten Son, Jesus gave His life for us, and He gave us His Spirit to accomplish His work.

Bill Bright taught us to follow the example of our Lord and to live a life of giving. The results of Campus Crusade for Christ's ministry have been possible because he and thousands of his staff members gave their lives as Christ's disciples, following the biblical admonition, "He died for all, that those who live should no longer live for themselves but for him who died for them and was raised again" (2 Corinthians 5:15 NIV).

Bill's life is an example of giving. He was always giving of himself—to the Lord, to family, to the ministry, to friends, and to anyone with whom he came in contact. In 1988, Bill and Vonette heard a telecast of a message I gave on stewardship, relating to giving financially. This touched Bill's heart and inspired him to give his entire retirement fund to establish a training center in Moscow. It turned out $50,000 was in the fund, and that was the exact amount needed for the training center! That was a thrill for Bill, and I was told he later had the opportunity to meet some of the people whose lives were dramatically changed as a result of attending training in that center.

Bill once said to me, "Would you help me with a campaign called 'I Found It, You Can Find It, Too'?" I thought, *This little, quiet man—what in the world is he up to?* But he finally convinced me, and so I did.

When we finished that campaign, he asked me, "Would you help me in this next crusade, 'Here's Life America'?" By then I had watched him, listened to him, prayed with him, and realized this was not a little man.

Bill Bright was a big man with a big vision, serving a big God, and he gave of himself in a big way to do what God had called him to do.

—CHARLES STANLEY

1

The Adventure of Giving

Deborah was a missionary serving overseas. Not long after she returned to the United States for her scheduled home leave, she learned that one of her neighbor's sons had been seriously injured. The family had no insurance and was suffering financially as well as physically.

Concerned about the situation, Deborah prayed, "Lord, what would You have me do?" She sensed God nudge her to give her neighbors some money. Checking her account, she realized that her balance was only $200.

"Lord, how about $25?" she prayed. With $175 left over, she thought she could survive the rest of the month. Quietly waiting on the Lord, however, she felt Him say, "No, I want you to give $100."

"I choked a bit," she said later. "That was half of what I had. As I continued to question the Lord, I had no peace about anything less than $100."

Finally, she wrote out a check, breathing a prayer. "Now I've done what You said, so You'll have to take care of my needs."

With a sense of joy and expectancy, Deborah took the check across the street. By this act of sharing, she greatly encouraged the family. And God kept His word. Two days later, Deborah received a check for $100 through the mail. Three days later, a woman dropped by with a check for $200—something she had wanted to do for some time, she told Deborah.

"Within five days of writing my check, I received from unexpected sources a total of $500," Deborah said. "I stood in awe of God and His ways."

She had discovered one of the greatest privileges and blessings of the Christian life—the wonderful adventure of giving by faith.

OUR ROLE IN GOD'S ECONOMY

What does *adventure* mean to you?

Does it mean driving a Formula One race car at two hundred miles per hour? Maybe it means going on an archaeological dig in South America or climbing an icy cliff in the Swiss Alps. Or does it mean going on safari through Africa surrounded by wild animals?

One thing is for sure: When most people think of having an adventure, the last idea likely to come to mind is giving away their time or money! But I'd like to share with you a perspective on giving that might change your view of it, a perspective that just might help you see your opportunities to give as nothing less than an exciting personal adventure.

Stewardship is at the core of all giving.

But first, let's talk a bit about stewardship. Stewardship is at the core of all giving. And in order to be a good steward of what God has given us, we must first gain an understanding of our role in His economy. Throughout Scripture, God promises us prosperity and abundance as we share that with which He trusted us. When asked what stewardship means, a young boy put it well: "It means that life is a ship loaded with a cargo of many things on its way to many people in many places," he said. "God is the Owner, but I am the captain of the ship, and He holds me responsible for the distribution."

In the New Testament, *steward* is described two different ways. One emphasizes guardianship over children and the administration of a master's household. The other stresses the role of a manager over property. In either case, a steward oversees another person's affairs and property.

Because not many of us have the resources to appoint a steward over our affairs, we are personally responsible. The decisions we make daily about spending and saving determine our effectiveness as a steward.

The average Christian is, however, ignorant of basic stewardship, while popular teachings about money mislead many sincere believers. As a result, the kingdom of God is losing vast sums of money and other valuable resources which could have helped change lives by the power of the risen Christ.

This book's basic premise is that most of what we give to God's work should have some relationship to fulfilling our Lord's Great Commission to "go into all the world and preach the good news to everyone, everywhere" (Mark 16:15 TLB). My goal is to help you discover how to invest wisely in God's kingdom and increase your fruitfulness for Christ.

We do not need to operate blindly or from ignorance in managing our stewardship. God has established principles valid for all time. I would like to help Christians understand the biblical basis for stewardship and to bring balance to the practice of giving. I want Christians to see how they can experience the abundant life assured by God's promised blessings if we follow those principles for giving. Finally, I want to encourage Christians to help fulfill the Great Commission by investing strategically and generously in the expansion of the kingdom of God.

When we do not follow these biblical principles, financial disaster lies ahead. One of the first questions that comes to my mind when I am counseling a person who has financial problems is, "Are you obeying the laws of God concerning stewardship?" I'm convinced these laws of God in the spiritual realm are as inviolate as the laws of the physical world. Ignorance of or disobeying these laws results in self-imposed poverty, both materially and spiritually. The person who disobeys God in stewardship cannot walk in the Holy Spirit's fullness and power. Neither can he know the joy of the Lord and the peace of Christ in his heart. The one who truly does what God tells him to do will experience the abundant life.

I'm sure all of us would like to experience true abundance. It's available! Our Lord said, "My purpose is to give life in all its fullness" (John 10:10 TLB).

The apostle John records, "I pray that in all respects you may prosper and be in good health, just as your soul prospers" (3 John v. 2 NASB). Psalm 1 says that if we delight ourselves in the Lord, meditate upon His Word day and night, and always seek ways to follow Him more closely, we are like trees along a riverbank bearing luscious fruit each season without fail. Our leaves will never wither, and all we do will prosper (Psalm 1:2–3). However,

When we do not follow these biblical principles, financial disaster lies ahead.

prosperity and our role as keepers of God's blessings frequently have been misunderstood.

Few people realize that Jesus had much to say about money—more than virtually any other subject. We need to learn what He taught us! Yet our responsibility as stewards extends beyond the administration of finances. Stewardship over all that God entrusts to us in life is foundational to giving. Our task, then, is to manage our time, talent, and treasure to bring glory to God.

GOD OWNS IT, WE MANAGE IT

All that we have, we own under God. Everything belongs to Him. He has never given us the absolute proprietorship in anything. The psalmist records, "The earth is the LORD's, and everything in it, the world, and *all* who live in it" (Psalm 24:1 NIV). Jesus Christ created us (Colossians 1:15–18). He bought us with His precious blood (1 Peter 1:18–19). God anointed Him as Lord (Ephesians 1:20–23). God's ownership is eternal and unchanging. He never has given up this right—and never will.

Foundational to all understanding of stewardship is that God entrusts us with the responsibilities of His kingdom. He has put into our hands the administration of all that He owns. The Christian steward realizes that in Christ "we live and move and have our being" (Acts 17:28 NIV). God is our preeminent Master. The whole of our life—our personality, influence, material substance, everything—is His, even our successes. He holds us accountable for how we manage what He has given us (Matthew 25:14–30; Romans 14:12).

This divine perspective helps us understand our purpose for living as Christians. Apart from the command to love God and others, His most important command is to "go into all the world" and "make disciples of all the nation" (Mark 16:15; Matthew 28:19). I am not here merely to enjoy the good life. I am here as a child and a servant of God to invest my time, my talent, and my treasure to seek and to save the lost. This is what our Lord came to do nearly two thousand years ago and what He commanded His followers to do generation after generation until His blessed return.

2

Qualifications of a Steward

rthur De Moss was a gifted and godly businessman. He built one of the most successful businesses of its kind in America and in the process gained a fortune of an estimated $500 million.

Then suddenly, during an economic recession, stock in his company plummeted. He lost $360 million in only four months—an average of $3 million a day, more than anybody had ever before lost in such a short amount of time. One would think he would have been devastated, needing to cut back on his Christian giving. Instead, he increased his giving. As we talked together during that period, Art was rejoicing in the Lord.

"The Lord gave me everything I have," he explained. "It all belongs to Him, and if He wants to take it away, that's His business. I don't lose any sleep. I still have a wonderful family, and my lifestyle remains unchanged. I will do anything God wants me to do. If He takes away everything He has entrusted to me and calls me to the mission field, I'm ready to go. All He needs to do is tell me."

Art placed his trust completely in his Lord and not in his fortune. God honored Art's faith and obedience and eventually restored all he had lost and much more. Art has now gone to be with the Lord, but his fortune is still being used for the glory of God.

Art's story illustrates an amazingly liberating principle of stewardship: If we faithfully use all that God entrusts to us, and if we keep His ownership of everything in our lives clearly in focus, any material loss simply represents His decision to direct to another the stewardship of that possession. This concept removes the burdensome grief associated with losing what we consider our own, since in fact it is not our own. In times of tragedy, God never forsakes us. He supplies all our needs. As stewards, our task is to trust Him completely.

What makes a good steward? Let's examine five important qualifications.

A GOOD STEWARD IS FAITHFUL

The apostle Paul wrote, "It is required in stewards that one be found faithful" (1 Corinthians 4:2 NKJV). Faithfulness is dependability—a steady, day-by-day obedience to what God has given us to do.

Faithfulness is dependability— a steady, day-by-day obedience to what God has given us to do.

Every morning when Vonette and I get on our knees before God, we remember that we belong to Him. We acknowledge that we love Him with all our hearts, with all our souls, and with all our minds. We ask Him to walk around in our bodies, to think with our minds, to love with our hearts, to speak with our lips. And since He came to seek and to save the lost, we ask Him to continue seeking and saving the lost through us. Throughout the day, we make decisions in light of this commitment.

Obedience to Scripture, persistence in claiming the promises of God's Word, a daily commitment to "walk in the light as He is in the light" (1 John 1:7 NKJV), and to abide in Christ and let His Word abide in us (John 15:1–8)—these are the qualities of a faithful steward.

A GOOD STEWARD IS TRUSTWORTHY

As faithfulness relates to dependability, trustworthiness means integrity. If you are honest, your word is your bond. The most important virtue in life is our integrity. As good stewards, our reputation, our character, our trustworthiness, our integrity must be above reproach.

As a boy, I learned that one's word outweighed any written contract. My grandfather and my father would complete large business deals involving large sums of money with a handshake. They took pride in their integrity. Once my grandfather had several associates who had invested in one of his oil properties. For some reason, that project did not develop as he had promised. Although he was not legally obligated, he felt constrained to return their funds. You do not always have control over your wealth, but you are the one who decides whether you can be trusted.

In 1948, while on my way to Oklahoma for my December 30 wedding to Vonette Zachary, I passed through the city of Okmulge where my grandfather had lived for many years. I had visited my grandparents there often. Suddenly, I remembered my need to purchase gifts for the wedding party and stopped at a jewelry store.

Before looking for the items I wanted, I asked the man in charge, whom I later learned was the owner, if he would cash an out-of-state check.

"I'm sorry, sir," he shook his head courteously. "It's against our policy."

I turned to walk out of the store.

"Do you know anyone in this city?" he called after me.

"No. My grandfather used to live here, but he's been dead for several years," I offered.

"What was his name?"

"Sam Bright."

"Are you the grandson of Sam Bright?" the man approached me with enthusiasm.

I nodded.

"Sam Bright was the most honorable man I have ever known!" he exclaimed. "If you're anything like your grandfather, I will sell you anything in this store. And I'll take your check!"

I felt moved by this experience. Although my grandfather had been gone for many years, he had left a legacy of integrity.

A GOOD STEWARD IS KNOWLEDGEABLE

In considering investments for our Lord, we must study various Christian enterprises to determine which merits our help.

Fund-appeal letters provide a good source of information. "Many Christians get tired of all those letters asking for money," a dear friend told me one day. "But I get excited about them. I'm always looking for a better opportunity to invest my money to serve the Lord. I don't hesitate to say yes if the project is a good investment for the kingdom."

I encourage you to seek the counsel of other godly

Christians who invest in worthwhile projects. Determine which churches and ministries best fulfill God's plan for your giving and investigate their track records. Ask for financial statements, and enclose with each request a contribution large enough to make the effort worthwhile. Find out how long the ministries have been in existence and what they have accomplished for the cause of Christ. Further, examine the credentials of those who lead the movements.

Common sense, or a "sound mind," is a good guide as well. Paul said to Timothy, "God has not given us a spirit of fear, but of power and of love and of a sound mind" (2 Timothy 1:7 NKJV). Apply this God-given sense. Invite the Holy Spirit to help you invest your money where you know it will bear the best results for His glory.

A Good Steward Is Effective in Ministry

The measure of good stewardship is fruitfulness. Let us look at a parable that Jesus told to illustrate this point:

> The kingdom of heaven "can be illustrated by the story of a man going into another country, who called together his servants and loaned them money to invest for him while he was gone.
>
> "He gave $5,000 to one, $2,000 to another, and $1,000 to the last—dividing it in proportion to their abilities—and then left on his trip. The man who received the $5,000 began immediately to buy and sell with it and soon earned another $5,000. The man with $2,000 went right to work, too, and earned another $2,000.
>
> "But the man who received the $1,000 dug a hole in the ground and hid the money for safekeeping.

"After a long time, their master returned from his trip and called them to him to account for his money. The man to whom he had entrusted the $5,000 brought him $10,000.

"His master praised him for good work. 'You have been faithful in handling this small amount,' he told him, 'so now I will give you many more responsibilities. Begin the joyous tasks I have assigned to you.'

"Next came the man who had received the $2,000, with the report, 'Sir, you gave me $2,000 to use, and I have doubled it.'

"'Good work,' his master said. 'You are a good and faithful servant. You have been faithful over this small amount, so now I will give you much more.'

"Then the man with the $1,000 came and said, 'Sir, I knew you were a hard man, and I was afraid you would rob me of what I earned, so I hid your money in the earth and here it is!'

A faithful steward will scrutinize his opportunities and invest ... [to] produce the best results.

"But his master replied, 'Wicked man! Lazy slave! Since you knew I would demand your profit, you should at least have put my money into the bank so I could have some interest.

Take the money from this man and give it to the man with the $10,000. For the man who uses well what he is given shall be given more, and he shall have abundance. But from the man who is unfaithful, even what little responsibility he has shall be taken from him.'"

MATTHEW 25:14–29 TLB

A faithful steward will scrutinize his opportunities and invest what God has given him in such a way that it will produce the best results.

Even in giving to our church, we should examine its fruitfulness. While studying your church budget, ask yourself these questions: What is my church doing to help fulfill the Great Commission? How many people is it introducing to Christ each year? How many of these are being discipled to grow and mature in their spiritual walk? Does my church show concern for orphans, widows, and other needy people?

The master in Jesus' parable held each steward responsible for his investment. He rewarded or rebuked the steward according to his fruitfulness. In like manner, our Lord expects fruitfulness in the "little things" of material wealth before He will entrust us with the true riches of eternal value (Luke 16:10–11 NLV).

A GOOD STEWARD IS GODLY

A good steward lives a godly life. Holiness is God's highest and most glorious attribute. Personal godliness begins with our birth into the family of God. We actually receive into our lives the One who is holy and perfect—the Lord Jesus, the risen Christ. From that moment, Christ begins to develop His life in us, a process that continues throughout our lives.

Some time ago, my heart grieved as I learned of a respected Christian leader who had fallen into a life of sin. He had obviously not intended to do so, but when the temptation came, he gave in. As a result, his wife, family, friends, and fellow Christians suffered severe heartache. Most tragically, his testimony and witness for Jesus have suffered untold damage. Many have ridiculed and rejected the cause of Christ because of his sin.

Since God wants us to live a holy life, the Enemy seeks to entrap us in sin and defeat. Several years ago a story in a national magazine described a couple who adopted two wolf cubs that they found while making a film about caribou in Alaska. They took the young wolves home and raised them with tender, loving care. For a while the wolves behaved just like friendly dogs. One day, however, they turned on their masters, who barely escaped with their lives. The wolves then fled to join a wild wolf pack. No matter how kindly their masters had treated them, their natures were such that sooner or later they would behave like other wolves.

> *Victory is assured only as we live ... under the power and control of the Holy Spirit.*

Similarly, our sinful nature stays the same. No amount of education, refinement, culture, or kindness can take away its selfishness and proneness to sin. Victory is assured only as we live moment by moment under the power and control of the Holy Spirit.

Christians who fall into carnal living do so because they fail to recognize the danger signals in their spiritual walk. The love of self, the love of pleasure, and the love of money consume and preoccupy them, affecting their giving, their priorities, and their intimacy with God himself. As a result, Satan robs them of their joy in Christ and destroys their witness as children of God.

How does one live a consistent godly life? God has given us His Holy Spirit to empower us for holy living and fruitful witness. He releases His power in our lives as we spend time daily in the presence of God through diligent Bible study and prayer, obey Him in all things and avoid those things that dishonor Him, claim His promises in the face of temptation, and keep short accounts with God.

STAYING FAITHFUL

From the beginning of my Christian life, God gave me a strong desire to live a holy life and become a fruitful witness for our Lord Jesus Christ. I really worked at this matter of being a Christian. I attended church several times each week, gave leadership to a witnessing group of more than a hundred young people, and served as a deacon in the church. I studied and memorized Scripture, lived a disciplined life of prayer, and witnessed for Christ regularly. Yet the harder I tried to live the Christian life, the more frustrated I became. I often felt guilty and spiritually inadequate.

One day, as I was reading His Word, God graciously showed me how simply one can appropriate the fullness and power of the Holy Spirit to live a godly and fruitful life. He revealed to me the concept I call "Spiritual Breathing," which has enabled me to experience the exciting, wonderful, and adventurous joy

❖

Christians who fall into carnal living do so because they fail to recognize the danger signals in their spiritual walk.

of walking in the Spirit ever since. Through the years, this concept has enabled millions of Christians around the world to experience God's love and forgiveness in their lives.

Spiritual Breathing, like physical breathing, is a process of "exhaling" the impure and "inhaling" the pure. Think for a moment on how your body needs to breathe. When you exhale, you rid your lungs of carbon dioxide and other impurities that would cause disease if they stayed in your system. Then, when you inhale, you breathe in the oxygen so crucial to maintaining a healthy body.

So it is with spiritual life. Through sin, we break our fellowship with God. As a result, we feel guilty and estranged from our Lord; we become complacent, discouraged, and depressed. An exercise in faith, Spiritual Breathing enables us to experience God's love and forgiveness as a way of life.

We "exhale" by confession, which means we agree with God that whatever we are doing that displeases Him is sin. Next, we acknowledge that Christ has paid the penalty for our sins by shedding His blood and dying on the cross. Then, we repent. We experience a change of attitude by turning away from our wrongdoing.

Having confessed our sins, we then "inhale" by appropriating the fullness of God's Spirit by faith. We invite Him to direct, control, and empower our life according to His promise in Acts 1:8, "You shall receive power when the Holy Spirit has come upon you" (NKJV).

Spiritual Breathing is the secret to living the Spirit-filled life moment by moment. The Spirit-filled life is one in which we surrender the control of the throne of our life to our risen Lord and draw on His power through the enabling of the Holy Spirit to live the Christian life. When we retake control of the throne by a deliberate sin, by worry and anxiety or unbelief, we need to breathe spiritually.

Is sin causing difficulty in your life? Has unconfessed sin begun to accumulate? I encourage you to keep short accounts with God. Whenever you find yourself retaking control of the throne of your life, breathe spiritually. Ask God to give you His power to gain victory over every form of sin, worry, anxiety— whatever you have confessed to Him. You will not only experience a fulfilled, happy life, but you will love our Lord more and thus be more effective as a steward of His blessings.

3

Attitudes of a Steward

One Monday morning a Christian handyman came to work feeling depressed. "What's the matter, George?" his boss asked.

George frowned. "Yesterday I put a quarter in the collection plate," he explained sadly. "That is, I thought I put a quarter in. But when I got home, I discovered that I had put in the five-dollar gold piece you gave me at Christmas."

"Why, George!" his boss exclaimed. "That is no misfortune. After all, that was a good deed, and God will reward you for it."

George shook his head slowly. "You can't fool the Lord. He knows that in my heart I wanted to give only twenty-five cents."

A steward's attitude is vital.

Paul admonishes, "Let everyone give as his heart tells him, neither grudgingly nor under compulsion, for God loves the man whose heart is in his gift."[1]

What attitudes of the heart are essential to being a good steward? Let's examine three.

1. A GOOD STEWARD IS OBEDIENT

Obedience to our heavenly Father is the natural and spiritual outgrowth of our faith. An attitude of obedience softens the soil of our hearts for fruitfulness in every good work and gives testimony to God's ownership of our possessions.

Our Lord's commands to give are many. "Give to him who asks you, and from him who wants to borrow from you do not turn away" (Matthew 5:42 NKJV). Jesus said, "Freely you have received, freely give ... Give to the poor ... Give alms of such things as you have ..." (Matthew 10:8; 19:21; Luke 11:41 NKJV).

In Matthew 25, our Lord tells us to feed the hungry and clothe the needy. He commands us to be hospitable to strangers, visit the sick, and minister to those in prison. Sharing with those in need, He teaches, is the same as giving to God (Matthew 25:33–40).

As we obey God, our example will encourage other Christians to abide by God's principles of stewardship. For instance, several years ago I met a young man of modest means who had heard about the Here's Life World strategy to help fulfill the Great Commission. He felt impressed to "adopt" the country of Thailand.

We needed about $75,000 for the Here's Life Thailand campaign. This man proceeded to sell a piece of property for which he received almost that exact amount. Even though this gift represented most of his savings, he felt impressed of God to pick up the entire cost for that country with the sale's proceeds.

Many of the volunteers who prepared to reach Bangkok during the Here's Life campaign took the gospel to other cities, villages, and hamlets of Thailand. Sometime later I went on a speaking tour of several Asian countries, including Thailand. While there I spoke at the dedication service of 258 Thais who had committed themselves to take the gospel to their country of 48 million. This all began through the obedient stewardship and sacrificial giving of one American. God used this story of dedication to inspire several other men to give to help fulfill the Great Commission in other countries through Here's Life World. Equally important, the young man's investment had, by 1989, helped to introduce more than 1.3 million people to Christ, set up more than 18,000 New Life Groups in homes, and start 3,338 churches. It is quite probable that apart from his original investment, the spiritual harvest now taking place in Thailand would not have been possible.

> *Whatever God enables us to earn and save during our lifetime, He expects us to use as good stewards.*

God has a particular plan for each of us. I cannot suggest to anyone what his lifestyle should be. I do know that God's Word commands us to seek first the kingdom of God and to set our affections on the things above (Matthew 6:33; Colossians 3:2). Whatever God enables us to earn and save during our lifetime, He expects us to use as good stewards.

Because of our old nature, we often hold back in our stewardship, fearing we will not have enough for our own needs. But God will not ask of us more than what we have or what He will provide. Nor will He ever ask us to give what is not ours to give.

If you and I and Christians everywhere simply will obey our Lord's command to lay up treasures in heaven, we will release vast sums of money to advance His kingdom. As a result, God's people will have the resources to reach millions of people for Christ and fulfill the Great Commission in this generation.

2. A GOOD STEWARD IS THANKFUL

An attitude of gratitude and thanksgiving also characterizes a good steward. The apostle Paul admonishes us to "always be thankful, for this is God's will for you who belong to Christ Jesus" (1 Thessalonians 5:18 TLB).

When we acknowledge our faith in Him through this attitude, even though circumstances seem hopeless, God releases His miraculous power and intervention on our behalf. He turns tragedy to triumph, discord to harmony, and defeat to victory.

Many years ago my personal world seemed to be crumbling around me. All that I had worked and planned for in the ministry of Campus Crusade for Christ was hanging by a slender thread. Because of a series of unforeseen circumstances, we were facing a financial crisis that could have bankrupted the movement, resulting in the loss of our beautiful facilities at Arrowhead Springs, California.

He turns tragedy to triumph, discord to harmony, and defeat to victory.

Years before, I had discovered that when we express faith through thanksgiving, obedience, and gratitude to God, He releases His great power on our behalf and enables us to be more fruitful for Him. So when the word came to me that everything was virtually lost, I fell to my knees and began to praise the Lord in faith.

As I thanked God in the midst of this crisis, His supernatural peace flooded my heart. I felt assured that He would provide the miracle we needed. In a matter of a few days, totally apart from any of my own abilities to solve the problem, God brought the right people into the right circumstances with the funds to save Arrowhead Springs for the ministry.

3. A GOOD STEWARD IS CHEERFUL AND JOYFUL

The apostle Paul counsels, "Every one must make up his own mind as to how much he should give. Don't force anyone to give more than he really wants to, for cheerful givers are the ones God prizes" (2 Corinthians 9:7 TLB).

The Greek word for "cheerful" is *hilaros*, from which we get the word "hilarious." Supernatural, Holy Spirit-directed stewardship is giving with expectation, excitement, joy, praise—even laughter. Indeed, God prizes "hilarious givers" because they are the ones who have discovered that it is truly "more blessed to give than to receive" (Acts 20:35).

Those Christians who give grudgingly or merely from a sense of duty lose the joy of stewardship. They do not realize that giving should be a natural expression of love and obedience to God, who promises to bless them abundantly.

An attitude of hilarious giving comes from our innermost being as a spontaneous response to what God has called us to do.

The story of Norm and Martha Barclay[2] illustrates this principle. When Martha was pregnant with her second child, Norm learned he was about to lose his job with an aviation firm. They had always given 10 percent of Norm's salary to the Lord's work, and they continued to do so even though they knew the layoff was coming. God faithfully honored their commitment, and only two days after his layoff Norm found a higher-paying job.

A few years later he suffered another totally unexpected layoff. Because of a recession, the prospects of finding another job seemed bleak.

———————❖———————

Those Christians who give grudgingly or merely from a sense of duty lose the joy of stewardship.

During this time, a guest speaker visited their church, and their Sunday school class took a special offering for him. Norm and Martha decided to give, and many in the class could not believe it. They were amazed that the Barclays were not hoarding every penny, but instead were expecting God to meet their needs. And He did; soon, Norm found a much better job, which enhanced his career.

After their children were grown and gone, Martha went to work for a Christian ministry. With two incomes, the Barclays decided to increase their giving considerably. God blessed them more materially, and they again increased their giving—even when Norm's job at times seemed unstable.

"God continues to supply our needs abundantly," Martha said. "We thoroughly love being able to give hilariously—it's one of the greatest joys we have."

———————————

1. Second Corinthians 9:7, *Letters to Young Churches: A Translation of the New Testament Epistles* by J. B. Phillips (New York: The Macmillian Company, 1957).

2. "Hilarious Giving," *Worldwide Challenge* (November/December 1984), p. 41.

4

Responsibilities of a Steward

Have you paused recently to reflect on God's greatness, to look upon Him in wonder, or to describe His glory to those around you? As stewards, our responsibility is to know the One who has given us our stewardship. Our primary task in managing all that God entrusts to us is to reflect His character in all that we do and say.

A GOOD STEWARD KNOWS GOD'S CHARACTER

Let me share with you nine attributes of God to help you reflect on and appreciate His unmatched greatness. This will enable you to more fully trust and obey Him and become a more pleasing and effective steward.

GOD IS SOVEREIGN AND ETERNAL

The Scriptures describe Him as the first and the last. He had no beginning. He will have no end. He owes His existence to no one. Above space and time, He provides a permanent foundation and a secure home and resting place for His children (1 Chronicles 29:11–12; Deuteronomy 33:27).

GOD IS OMNIPRESENT

Unlimited by space, He is everywhere. His presence fills the heavens and the earth (Jeremiah 23:24). God is ever with us to comfort us, to fellowship with us, to give us boldness in telling others about Him.

GOD IS OMNIPOTENT

He is all-powerful and the provider and sustainer of all things (Jeremiah 32:17). As the Creator, He involves Himself intimately in the affairs of men.

GOD IS OMNISCIENT

He knows everything (Romans 11:33–34). His Word teaches us there is no place in the universe we can go that will separate us from Him. Nothing escapes His attention or catches Him by surprise.

GOD IS HOLY

He alone is completely pure and free from iniquity (Exodus 15:11). Totally committed to goodness, He is at war with evil. Because God's holiness cannot tolerate sin, wrongdoers cannot live in His presence until the blood of our Savior and Lord Jesus Christ has cleansed them.

GOD IS LOVE

He expressed the depth of His love by the cross. God's holiness and moral purity demand punishment for sin. He is long-suffering and patient, however, preferring to give people the opportunity to repent and accept His forgiveness through Christ.

GOD IS TRUTHFUL

His truth is the foundation of all knowledge (John 14:6). It does not change or accommodate itself to varying cultures and standards. Truth is essential to God himself—it has always existed and always will.

GOD IS MERCIFUL

Paul writes, "God is so rich in mercy ... that even while we were dead because of our sins, he gave us life when he raised Christ from the dead" (Ephesians 2:4–5).

GOD IS TRUSTWORTHY

His truth is inseparable from His character. God cannot mislead or lie, for this would violate His nature. Honesty and integrity are essential to God himself.

Knowing God and seeking Him more fully enable us to recognize that at any time and in any place He will be our strength to be a faithful steward. (For an inspiring study of the attributes of God, let me recommend *The Joy of Trusting God*, the first book in "The Joy of Knowing God" series.)

A GOOD STEWARD BELIEVES IN "MULTIPLICATION"

I often recall the statement "Born to reproduce." God has given to His children a miraculous method called spiritual multiplication for taking the message of His love and forgiveness in Christ to every living person.

The amazing pattern of a strawberry plant beautifully illustrates this concept. Extending from the main vine are several wiry green stems, like arms shooting out in different directions. Each of these slender stems reaches across six inches of soil until it penetrates the earth and forms roots of its own. Thus each stem becomes a new strawberry plant.

Until this baby plant sustains itself, it draws life and nourishment from the mother plant via the runner. Once it establishes itself and matures, however, the newborn plant begins to sprout its own runners, replicating itself many more times over.

Spiritual multiplication simply means winning people to Christ, building them in their Christian faith, then sending them out to win and disciple others for our Lord Jesus, generation after generation.

A GOOD STEWARD
MANAGES TIME, TALENT, AND TREASURE

A faithful steward also manages his time, talent, and treasure for maximum effectiveness in doing God's will.

USING TIME WISELY

Perhaps you have heard the story about the farmer who told his wife he was going out to plow the "south forty." He got off to an early start so he could oil the tractor. He needed more oil, so he went to the shop to get it. On the way he noticed the pigs needed feeding. So he proceeded to the corncrib, where he found some sacks of feed. The sacks reminded him that his potatoes were sprouting. Then when he started for the potato pit, he passed the woodpile and remembered that his wife wanted wood in the house. As he picked up a few sticks, an ailing chicken passed by. He dropped the wood and picked up the chicken. When evening arrived, the frustrated farmer had not even gotten to the tractor, let alone to the field.

Have you ever intended to do something you knew was

important but found yourself distracted by other tasks that kept you from accomplishing your main goal?

Time is a gift of God, and we must use it wisely. We read in Ephesians 5, "Be careful how you walk, not as unwise men but as wise, making the most of [or

> *Time is a gift of God, and we must use it wisely.*

redeeming] your time, because the days are evil" (vv. 15–16 NASB). God knows what we have to accomplish today.

STEWARDSHIP OF TALENT

The stewardship of our talent matters equally. The Holy Spirit has endowed each of us with at least one spiritual gift (1 Corinthians 12:7), and we would be poor stewards if we ignored that special ability.

Often people have asked me, "What is the difference between a spiritual gift and natural ability?" The difference is not always clear. All spiritual gifts and natural abilities come from God. Whether our ability stems from a spiritual gift or a natural talent really is not important—God expects us to develop that gift or talent to its fullest potential through the control and empowering of the Holy Spirit. He requires us to exercise much discipline and hard work as we use our talent according to God's will and for His glory.

WHERE IS YOUR TREASURE?

Matthew 6:21 records perhaps the simplest truth about our commitment to stewardship, "Where your treasure is, there your heart will be also" (NASB).

One can determine much about a Christian's spiritual life by what he treasures. Our use of money clearly shows our spiritual commitment because where our heart is, our treasure will follow.

A GOOD STEWARD CARES FOR SOULS

A steward is also the guardian of human souls, a concept seldom considered in the context of stewardship.

The only treasure you will have in heaven is what you lay up through your efforts for God here on earth. The greatest treasures of all will be the souls we bring to Jesus Christ through the investment of our time, talent, and treasure. Although people have turned away from God, they are still God's creation. God has chosen to use human instruments to bring repentant individuals back to Himself. By bringing a nonbeliever into our lives, God grants us the joyful opportunity of stewardship in reclaiming that soul for Him. It is extraordinary that God would choose us to do the most important thing possible. Anything we can do, including giving to God's work in saving others, is the greatest joy imaginable—and we need to see it as such.

God grants us the joyful opportunity of stewardship in reclaiming souls for Him.

How can we be faithful stewards of souls?

PRAY FOR THE LOST

Think of someone you know who needs Christ, and pray specifically for that person. Ask the Holy Spirit to send someone across your path who needs to hear God's message of love and forgiveness. Pray for the power and boldness you will need to speak to that individual.

Price: $14.99

Title: The Joy of Dynamic Giving

Author: Dr. Bill Bright

ISBN: 0781442540

Publisher: Cook Communications Ministries

Date: 10-05-05

TRUST THE HOLY SPIRIT TO PREPARE THE PERSON'S HEART

Whenever I am with a person for even a few minutes, I consider it a divine appointment. I believe God has brought us together because that person needs to hear the gospel.

Being a steward of souls is like being a good businessman. He always has his antenna out for anything that looks like a better investment for his dollar. If I neglect a divine appointment, I am not a good steward of that opportunity. A good steward of souls will get up in the morning and say, "Now, Lord, who do You want me to talk to today?" All day long—on a plane, in the office, or out on the campus—he is ever sensitive to the leading of the Holy Spirit.

DRAW ON THE POWER OF THE HOLY SPIRIT

Tell others about Jesus, confident that the Holy Spirit is helping you. If you have never received training in how to tell others about Christ, let me suggest you read *Witnessing Without Fear: How to Share Your Faith With Confidence* (Thomas Nelson, 1993). In this book, I share a proven, step-by-step approach that will help you witness effectively for our Lord. Another helpful resource is *The Joy of Sharing Jesus*, part of "The Joy of Knowing God" series.

LEAVE THE RESULTS TO GOD

Many will listen to the gospel and gladly receive the Lord; others will reject Him. But don't get discouraged. Even Jesus was unable to bring everyone to whom He spoke into His kingdom. Our task is simply to take the initiative to share. God must change the person's heart.

We have all heard the popular expression "You can't take it with you." When Howard Hughes died, someone asked, "How much money did he leave?" Another replied, "All of it." We cannot take our material possessions with us. For all eternity we will enjoy riches we do not deserve. The one thing we will not have in heaven is the priceless privilege of introducing souls to our Savior. As fruitful Christian stewards here on earth, however, we will take with us to heaven every soul we have brought to Christ. We can take eternal things into eternity. That's something to be very joyful about.

5

Why Giving Makes Sense

The Bible records more than seven hundred references to giving. The New Testament has more to say about it than about the return of Christ. From earliest youth to oldest age, rich or poor, we are all commanded by God to give. So as we continue to explore the joy of dynamic giving, let's focus on several reasons why a spirit of giving makes sense.

GIVING BEGAN WITH GOD

God's supernatural expression of giving was in the sacrifice of His only begotten Son that we might receive forgiveness for our sins, become children of God, and enjoy eternal life. God continues to give of Himself today in love, forgiveness, peace, purpose, and power. By this He enables us to live full, meaningful lives. The source of all life, He continues among other things to provide us with food, air, water, shelter, and clothing.

GIVING IS A LAW OF GOD

After the flood, God made a covenant that "while the earth remains, seedtime and harvest ... shall not cease" (Genesis 8:22 NKJV). From the beginning, the law of the harvest has governed nature and formed the means for God's abundant blessings. When our Lord said, "Give, and it will be given to you," He was referring to this principle. Giving is not optional for the believer. Jesus commanded us to "give to him who asks you, and from him who wants to borrow from you do not turn away" (Matthew 5:42 NKJV). He also said, "Freely you have received, freely give" (Matthew 10:8 NKJV).

GIVING WAS THE LIFESTYLE OF OUR LORD

A concise description of Jesus' lifestyle appears in the book of Acts, which records, "He went about doing good" (10:38 NASB). Jesus gave in feeding the multitudes. He gave in healing the sick. He gave in teaching His disciples. He gave in empowering His disciples for evangelism. He gave in compassion for the poor. He gave in offering rest to the weary. He gave in dying on the cross for our sins. He gave in sending His Holy Spirit.

Our Lord spoke about giving as much as, if not more than, any other subject. Half of His recorded parables concern our stewardship of money, property, time, skills, and relationships with others in dealing with material possessions. He taught us that the secret to abundance is to "give, and it will be given to you: good measure, pressed down, shaken together, and running over will be put into your bosom" (Luke 6:38 NKJV).

GIVING IS THE ESSENCE OF BEING

I have often shared the story of a baby girl who lay near death, critically injured in an automobile accident. She desperately needed a blood transfusion, but doctors could find no one who had her rare blood type. In the midst of their frantic search, the doctors discovered that the child's older brother, Kevin, had the right type. Anxious to proceed, one of the doctors sat down with the seven-year-old boy and talked quietly with him.

"Your sister is very sick, son," he said somberly. "If we don't help her, she's not going to live. I want to know if you are willing to give your blood to help your baby sister?"

His face pale with fear, Kevin seemed to struggle with his answer. Then, after a few moments, he said softly, "Yes, I will."

The little boy watched sadly and silently as his blood flowed from his arm through the tube.

"We're almost finished," the doctor smiled encouragingly.

Kevin's eyes filled with tears. "How long till I die?" he whispered.

Looking at him in amazement, the doctor realized that Kevin thought he was to give all his blood to save his sister. That brave little boy had believed that his act of mercy would cost him his life, yet he was willing to do it!

I wonder: How far are we willing to go in helping others? How much of ourselves are we willing to give?

GIVING IS THE BASIS OF RECEIVING

There is a vast difference between giving to receive and receiving because we give. We cannot manipulate or bribe God. In giving, we cannot say, "Ten will get me a hundred," or, to put it crudely, "God, my pocket is flat, so here's a buck to make it fat." He will not honor such an attitude.

Giving is the basis of receiving because it is a law of God. Only what we give to God can He multiply back to us in the form of supply (Luke 6:38). Multiplication is the mathematics of heaven. God commanded Adam and Eve to "be fruitful and multiply" (Genesis 1:28 NKJV). In His covenant with Abraham, God promised, "I will multiply your descendants as the stars of the heaven and as the sand which is on the seashore" (Genesis 22:17 NKJV). The apostle Paul records that God can "supply and multiply the seed you have sown" (2 Corinthians 9:10 NKJV). On two occasions our Lord multiplied a few loaves and fish to feed the multitudes that followed Him (Matthew 15:32; John 6:1–13). Whatever we give becomes the basis of God's multiplication because He applies the law of sowing and reaping to giving (2 Corinthians 9:6–10; Luke 6:38; Galatians 6:7).

GIVING BRINGS BLESSING

Money symbolizes our skill and effort in life. When we give of our possessions, we are essentially giving of ourselves. In the process we become channels of blessing.

The Sea of Galilee is a good example of this because as it receives and passes on its fresh, sweet water, the sea is a source of life. The surrounding plains are among the most fertile in the world.

A harp-shaped lake in the Jordan valley, the Sea of Galilee is fed by the Jordan River, which exits through a broad fertile valley at the southern tip of the lake. The region produces abundant crops of wheat, barley, fruit, and vegetables. Wildflowers and oleanders fringe the shoreline. The region was an important center of New Testament events, and Christ performed a third of His recorded miracles there (Mark 1:32–34; 3:10; 6:53–56).

By contrast, the Dead Sea—just sixty-five miles downstream—is a harsh, saline body of water. Like the Sea of Galilee, its freshwater source is the Jordan. Unlike the Sea of Galilee, however, the Dead Sea has no outlet. As a result, the water is bitter to taste and nauseous to smell.

The sea is so salty and so saturated with minerals, one can literally lie on his back in the water and read a newspaper. I did this once when I was visiting there. The surrounding area is a barren chaos of crags and wadis where even the Bedouin flocks find little sustenance, reinforcing the effect of lifeless shores around a lifeless sea. This intensely salty lake would be fresh or only mildly saline if it had an outlet.

Two bodies of water—one sweet and overflowing with blessing; the other bitter and lifeless. One receives and gives; the other receives and hoards.

Traveling the world, I have observed many Christians who can be typified by these waters. Like the Sea of Galilee, some are refreshed by "rivers of living water" (John 7:38). They give abundantly to the work of our Lord with enthusiasm and excitement. They are prosperous and filled with joy, "abounding in the work of the Lord" (1 Corinthians 15:58 NKJV).

I also have seen those who hang on to what God has entrusted to them, trying to build larger and larger estates. These people are usually cantankerous, negative, unhappy, and antisocial. What joy they have missed because, like the Dead Sea, their channel became blocked by greed and selfishness!

GIVING MINISTERS TO THE LORD JESUS

When we perform loving acts for others, our Lord records each kindness as if we had done it for Him personally. Our heavenly Father considers the smallest gesture—even a cup of cold water given to a thirsty person in His name—to be a gift from us to His beloved Son.

GIVING REMOVES STUMBLING BLOCKS TO FAITH

In presenting the gospel of our Lord Jesus Christ to others, sometimes we meet those who are hungry, out of work, sick, or burdened with other problems. What should be our response to their needs? Share Christ and be on our way? It is difficult, if not impossible, for them to listen to our witness until we translate our faith in Christ into loving care for their necessities. The apostle James says:

> What does it profit, my brethren, if someone says he has faith but does not have works? … If a brother or sister is naked and destitute of daily food, and one of you says to them, "Depart in peace, be warmed and filled," but you do not give them the things which are needed for the body, what does it profit? … I will show you my faith by my works.
>
> JAMES 2:14–18 NKJV

As we meet the special needs of those in distress, their hearts will be more open to receive God's love and forgiveness. This would enable us to do the most valuable work of all—introducing them to our wonderful Savior.

WHY IT'S SO BLESSED TO GIVE

The law of Spirit-directed giving applies to everyone. God desires to bless His children abundantly and promises to do so, if only we will demonstrate faith in Him through trust and obedience. Are you having difficulty meeting your financial obligations and providing food for your family? One of the best things you can do is find someone who has greater needs than you and share out of your meager resources. In the process, Paul says, "God is able to make it up to you by giving you everything you need and more, so that there will not only be enough for your own needs, but plenty left over to give joyfully to others" (2 Corinthians 9:8 TLB).

The book of Acts records the words of the Lord Jesus, "It is more blessed to give than to receive" (20:35). I remember I first heard this as a growing lad, then as an agnostic, and later as a young Christian. I could not comprehend how giving could be better than receiving. Now that I have been a Christian for many years, I truly understand. It is "more blessed to give" than to receive for several reasons.

GOD CREATED US WITHIN THE CONTEXT OF A GIVING UNIVERSE

When one chooses to contradict God's design, he or she suffers the consequences: greed, competitiveness, gross shortages, imbalances of wealth distribution, and insecurity.

GIVING IS MORE PRODUCTIVE

When we give freely of ourselves and of our possessions as a material expression of our spiritual obedience to Christ, God in turn meets our needs in abundance.

The story of a Christian newspaper reporter whose family was experiencing a severe financial need illustrates this point.

During an appeal for a special project at his church, the reporter felt impressed to give. Uncertain about the amount, he prayed, "Lord, how much should I give?"

The reply flashed into his mind as clearly as though it were spoken aloud: "You may give anything between $10 and $25."

Reaching for his checkbook, he scrawled $20 on a check and dropped it into the offering bag as it passed. A deep sense of peace settled over him as he began to trust God to supply his own need.

A short time later, the reporter and his wife put their house up for sale. The real estate agent shook his head as he wrote up the listing. "You'll never sell it at that price," he warned.

In less than two weeks, however, the couple had two buyers, each at full price. "By the time our negotiations ended," they testified, "we had a guaranteed sale at $2,000 above market value. Then, we realized what God had done. He had multiplied our $20 a hundredfold."

Meanwhile, the reporter had felt led to give another Christian ministry a gift of $13. Again, trusting God to supply his own need, he wrote out a check for the amount and dropped it in the mail. In the weeks to come, God miraculously enabled him to save $1,300 on the purchase of another home.

GIVING BEGINS AN ENDLESS CIRCLE OF JOY

God gives; we receive. We give; He receives. He then multiplies what we have given back to us in the form of our supply.

If we are giving to glorify God, we can expect a return that is more than the gift. The purpose of the return is that we may have the ability to give again, thus completing the circle.

Giving by faith is a principle basic to Spirit-directed

stewardship. Simply defined, giving by faith is taking God at His Word and giving generously as He provides.

The premise of this concept is threefold. First, God is the absolute source of our supply. Second, giving is based on His resources, not our own. Third, Christ is our link to God's inexhaustible riches. The apostle Paul includes these precepts in his letter to the Christians at Philippi: "My God shall supply all your need according to His riches in glory by Christ Jesus." (Philippians 4:19 NKJV).

God shall supply. Living in a humanistic society, it is easy to believe that humanity is our source of wealth. When in need, we look to people and to institutions for help. Indeed, God uses them in His process of provision, but they are the instruments—not the source—of our supply.

In placing our trust in people or things, it does not take long to discover their limitation in helping us. Acknowledging God as the total source of all that we need gives us a clear vision of His greatness and power to provide.

According to His riches. Our heavenly Father holds the treasures of heaven and earth in His hands. His supply is not based on the size of our need, but on the enormity of His riches. In good times and bad, His reserve remains stable and inexhaustible.

As God's stewards, we have opportunity to reflect His bountiful wealth. At times God will impress us to give what we cannot give. Then we must call upon His "riches in glory" rather than depend on our limited reservoir.

By Christ Jesus. We appropriate God's abundant blessings through Christ. The apostle Paul records, "Though he was so very rich, yet to help you he became so very poor, so that by being poor he could make you rich" (2 Corinthians 8:9 TLB).

Our Lord laid aside His riches in heaven to identify with us in every area of our human need. When He returned to His Father, God reinvested Him with all that He had laid aside— His infinite power, His unspeakable glory, and His inexhaustible riches.

As children of God, we identify with the death, burial, and resurrection of our Lord. By miraculous intervention, God placed us in Christ. When Jesus died on the cross, we died. When He arose from the grave, we arose. When He ascended into heaven, we ascended. Now, we sit with Him in the heavenly realms as joint heirs with Christ, blessed with "every spiritual blessing in the heavenly realms because we belong to Christ" (Ephesians 2:6; 1:3).

The moment we accepted Christ as our Savior and Lord, we received this inheritance. Because of our Lord's glorified position in heaven, and since He is with us now through His Holy Spirit, we have all sufficiency in Him.

If we ever plan to do anything for Christ and His kingdom, we must do it now. Growing worldwide problems and unprecedented opportunities for Christian ministry make giving an urgent priority.

Every Christian is responsible to help reach his own generation for Jesus Christ. We cannot be casual or indifferent about our task. We would make every effort to rescue a drowning person; let us place the same importance upon our time, talents, and treasure in taking the message of Christ to everyone who will listen (Colossians 1:28).

6

The Law of the Harvest

Every year, America's hardworking farmers harvest billions of bushels of barley, corn, oats, wheat, and rye. Assuming proper soil and weather conditions, they reap bountifully in the fall many times more than what they planted in the spring.

God's provision is based on the law of the harvest. This law is as inviolate as the law of gravity. As sure as the sun will rise and set tomorrow, one can be certain, "Whatever a man sows, that he will also reap" (Galatians 6:7 NKJV).

The law of the harvest is governed by five basic principles of sowing. When applied spiritually, ignoring these axioms can devastate our life and witness. By obeying them, however, we can experience life in all of its fullness as our Lord intended.

PRINCIPLE 1: PLANT SEEDS

Everything begins with a seed. Whatever we give will return to us because what we give is a seed we sow. God established this precept long ago. On the third day of creation, He commanded, "Let the earth burst forth with every sort of grass and seed-bearing plant, and fruit trees with seeds inside the fruit, so that these seeds will produce the kinds of plants and fruits they come from" (Genesis 1:11 TLB). Like begets like. To grow vegetables, we must plant vegetable seeds. To produce wheat, we must plant kernels of wheat. To reap anything, we must first plant a seed. Certainly, we cannot underestimate the incredible ability of even the smallest kernel.

This principle applies spiritually as well as physically. The apostle Paul said, "Whatever a man sows, that he will also reap. For he who sows to his flesh will of the flesh reap corruption, but he who sows to the Spirit will of the Spirit reap everlasting life" (Galatians 6:7–8 NKJV)

PRINCIPLE 2: PLANT THE BEST SEEDS

To reap a bountiful harvest, we must sow our best seed. Farmers know this principle well. A Midwestern wheat farmer faithfully supplied his neighbors with all the seed they needed to plant. Each year he would give them his choice seed and refuse to accept payment, insisting that they plant only what he supplied. After several years, the farmers finally learned why.

"I give you my best seed every year because I know that what you plant will affect my harvest. My farm is between the rolling hills on which your wheat grows. When our grain begins to grow, pollination occurs. If you don't plant the highest quality of grain, my quality of return is also affected. I give my best so I can harvest the best."

Every Christian should seek to maximize his time, talent, and treasure with training and good counsel to produce the greatest spiritual harvest. Many Christians are unhappy and miserable as stewards because they do not first give God their best, in obedience to the law of the harvest. The best of our time, talent, treasure—the best of everything we have—should be on the altar of sacrifice to God.

PRINCIPLE 3: SOW RIGHTEOUSLY

An abundant harvest springs from the most fertile soil. No intelligent farmer would consider planting inferior seed in poorly prepared soil using worn-out equipment. Rather, he would buy choice seed and prepare the soil thoroughly with the finest equipment and fertilizers available.

The best of our time, talent, treasure—the best of everything we have—should be on the altar of sacrifice to God.

The quality of the ground and its preparation are vital. Ideally, the soil must be heavy enough not to be easily eroded by the wind, yet light enough to mix well when tilled. Cultivation is crucial as well. The soil must be tilled until soft enough for planting, but not so loose that it will dry out. Tilling also rids the soil of weeds, which rob moisture from the seedlings and prevent the sunlight from producing strong, healthy plants.

The soil in which our financial giving develops also is vital. I marvel at the lifestyle of the average Christian, which differs little from that of nonbelievers in attitudes, actions, motives, desires, and words. All of this concerns the type of soil in which we plant our seed. Many Christians, even those who give faithfully, experience financial problems, emotional turmoil, even physical illness, because they are sowing poor seed in the unproductive soil of wrongful motives and unworthy enterprises.

Like planting good seed in fertile ground, our task as stewards is to sow righteously. "Sow with a view to righteousness, reap in accordance with kindness," admonished Hosea (Hosea 10:12 NASB).

We cannot appraise good stewardship by the amount of our gifts, but by how well we put them to good use. Rooted in fertile soil, righteous giving measures the stewardship of any gift by how well it reflects the will of God. Giving for the sake of giving, or contributing where our gifts are likely to be used for unrighteous purposes, is not only poor stewardship, but also contrary to the will of God. In the parable of the talents (Matthew 25:14–20; Luke 19:12–27), the nobleman did not fault the unrighteous steward because he failed to maximize the return on his investment. Rather, he denounced the steward because he did not properly use his money.[1]

Righteous stewardship is a function of knowledge. Wherever we give, we must determine whether our gift will be used for the glory of God. The local church, a well-known Christian ministry, or a popular charity does not necessarily qualify automatically. Since our Lord came to seek and to save the lost and He has commissioned us to do the same, the most fertile ground for giving is the soil that produces a harvest of fruitful disciples to help fulfill the Great Commission.

PRINCIPLE 4: EXPECT A GREAT RETURN

If we sow our best seed in the most fertile soil, we can expect an abundant return. The axiom of abundant return is simple: The crop is always abundantly more than its seed.

A single redwood tree can reproduce itself millions of times during its lifetime. A lone grape seedling is capable of branching into a prolific vine filled with luscious fruit. One peach pit will sprout into a huge tree laden with its delicious produce.

I believe that if every Christian understood the law of sowing and reaping, the Christian world would experience a dramatic, revolutionary change.

One often hears the expressions "You can't out give God" and "I gave by the spoonful, but God returned to me by the shovelful." God will never be in our debt. He designed the crop to be more than the seed. As we sow obediently and joyfully in faith and righteousness to our Lord, we can expect His abundant return.

PRINCIPLE 5: DIE TO SELF

To bear fruit, however, a seed must die. Planted in the ground, a kernel of wheat goes through an amazing metamorphosis. Dying in the process, it loses its own identity and gives up its previous existence. Life cannot spring from a dead seed, however. A change must take place. The seed must germinate to produce its seedling. The rain comes, and the hard, outer shell begins to soften under the pressure. The secret life

"He who loves his life will lose it, and he who hates his life in this world will keep it for eternal life" (John 12:25 NKJV).

buried inside the kernel begins to swell and eventually splits the shell and cracks it open. Only by this dissolution can the seed sprout and send forth abundant fruit. Thus life rises out of apparent death to produce its abundant harvest.

This principle also applies to stewardship. Our Lord said, "He who loves his life will lose it, and he who hates his life in this world will keep it for eternal life" (John 12:25 NKJV). This love-hate paradox teaches that we must be so committed to Christ and controlled and empowered by His Holy Spirit that we die to self. Any love outside this commitment is idolatrous and marked for failure.

Anything in life can become an idol. Money, cars, TV, home, hobbies, career, ministry, social calendar, friends, family—the list is endless. When possessed with worldly desires and ungodly ambitions, they supplant our love for the Lord. To be fruitful stewards we must die to the selfish attitudes that create these idols.

New attitudes will rise out of the death of our selfishness. Through Spiritual Breathing, the hard shell of our self-centeredness will soften and dissolve, enabling the Holy Spirit to create within us a renewed love for our Lord. This love will produce a bountiful harvest of godly motives, fruitful goals, and Spirit-directed priorities.

---

1. Gerald R. Thompson, "The Biblical Foundation for a Planned Giving Program," an unpublished essay, CBN University, 1987, p. 12.

7

The Goal of Giving

A lighthouse keeper worked on a treacherous stretch of rocky coastline many years ago. He took immaculate care of the huge lamp that warned the ships. Once a month, he replenished his supply of oil to keep the lamp burning.

The lighthouse keeper enjoyed his work, especially since he was not far from shore and had many guests drop in for visits. Having plenty of time to talk, he got to know the local villagers well.

One cold night, a widow who had several small children begged him to give her a little oil so she could keep her family warm. Touched by her desperate plea, he poured out a small amount into her jar.

Another night, a father brought his children to visit the lighthouse keeper. Preparing to leave, the father realized that he needed more oil for his lantern so he and his children could find their way back home. Later, someone else needed some oil to lubricate a wheel to avoid an accident. A compassionate man, the lighthouse keeper granted each legitimate request.

Toward the end of the month, his supply of oil ran dangerously low. Since he had never given out a large quantity to any one person, he was surprised. He tried to conserve what he had left, but soon it was gone and his beacon light went out.

As keepers of God's resources, we have but one purpose—to glorify Him.

That very night, several ships were wrecked, and many people drowned in the choppy waters.

Authorities investigated the incident and questioned the lighthouse keeper. Although he was repentant and sobbed in remorse, they were unsympathetic. "You were given oil for one purpose only—to keep that light burning! There is no excuse."

As keepers of God's resources, we have but one purpose also—to glorify Him. It is easy to let the day-to-day demands on our finances turn our eyes from this aim unless we clearly define our priorities. God's holy Word does this for us. The biblical order is God, our family, the church, and society.

PRIORITY 1: GOD

Our top priority is to love and obey God. Our Lord said, "You shall love the LORD your God with all your heart, with all your soul, and with all your mind. This is the first and great commandment. And the second is like it: 'You shall love your neighbor as yourself.' On these two commandments hang all the Law and the Prophets" (Matthew 22:37–40 NKJV).

Putting God and the fulfillment of our Lord's Great Commission first in our time, talents, and treasure must be the goal of our stewardship. Once this is so, all else falls into place.

PRIORITY 2: FAMILY

Under God, our family is number one. Since it was the first institution formed by our Creator (Genesis 1:27–28), no conflict exists between the preeminence of God and the priority of family. Rather, meeting the needs of our family is a scriptural mandate and an evidence of faith.

The apostle Paul admonishes, "If anyone does not provide for his own, and especially for those of his household, he has denied the faith and is worse than an unbeliever" (1 Timothy 5:8 NASB). An individual who neglects his family's needs to give to many organizations and causes is a poor testimony to the love and care that our heavenly Father has for His children. This principle applies equally to the stewardship of one's time and the sharing of one's companionship.

Within the hierarchy of the family, the needs of the spouse come first, followed by the children, the extended family, and, finally, one's self.

THE SPOUSE

As a husband, I am responsible to love Vonette as Christ loved the church (Ephesians 5:25), and that is a big commitment. Loving the Lord Jesus with all my heart, soul, mind, and strength—my absolute highest objective—enhances my love for her. Often, I must work eighteen to twenty hours a day. In the early years of this ministry, my schedule kept me away from home much of the time while Vonette cared for our sons.

Now that Zachary and Brad are grown and both are serving the Lord, Vonette and I usually travel together. In all these years, I have never lost sight of her as my first family priority. I try to let her know how important she is to me by the little niceties I do for her and by telling her often how very much I love her. When we are together, I try to be patient, loving, compassionate, and sensitive to her needs, not judgmental or critical. I do not take our relationship for granted but try to show my love for her in tangible and practical ways.

THE CHILDREN

Giving priority to our spouse's needs does not mean we can neglect our children. They are a gift from God (Psalm 127:3), and He expects us to love them and care for their needs. The psalmist records, "Just as a father has compassion on his children, so the LORD has compassion on those who fear Him" (Psalm 103:13 NASB). As parents, we model God's loving care by the way we provide for our children.

> As parents, we model God's loving care by the way we provide for our children.

Provision goes beyond their financial needs, of course. Children need a caring, touching atmosphere in which parents prove their love. Although spending time with our children is essential, it is how we treat them when we are together that counts. Parents who are patient, loving, understanding, and sensitive to their children demonstrate how important the children are.

EXTENDED FAMILY

The responsibility for the family goes beyond the immediate members to include the extended family—mother, father, and grandparents. Unfortunately, many Christians give generously of their time, abilities, and finances to their churches or businesses while their extended families live on the edge of poverty and starve from lack of attention, love, and care. God requires us to take care of our own and not to rely on the government, which has neither the understanding nor the resources to provide adequately.

ONE'S SELF

Personal care also is vital. To give more effectively to others, we must refresh ourselves spiritually and physically. If we are good stewards of our health and appearance, we will be more effective in our Christian witness.

Attention to our own needs does not mean "looking out for number one." Truly happy people care for the needs of others, trusting God to provide for their own necessities. Personally, I live modestly and do not see the need to accumulate a lot of things. As a faithful steward, I must wear the cloak of materialism loosely. My possessions do not own me. I control them and determine how to use them to accomplish the most for the glory of God.

PRIORITY 3: THE LOCAL CHURCH

Our stewardship to the church provides a support base for local evangelism, the church staff, and world missions.

The church that faithfully exalts our Lord and proclaims His holy, inspired Word is God's primary institution for worship and outreach to a spiritually needy world. As stewards of God's resources, we must help advance the cause of Christ through His local body. We must give whatever we can to edify the church, whether through our tithes and offerings or by teaching Sunday school, serving on various committees, participating in the evangelism and visitation programs, or washing windows on church workday.

By giving to the needs of the church—the mortgage, utilities,

salaries and honorariums, and other legitimate expenses—
we create a support base for evangelism. Blindly putting
money into the collection plate, however, is not good stewardship. We must be sure, without being too critical or
analytical, that our shepherds spend the budget properly and
that they do not compromise the church's vision.

CHURCH OUTREACH

As a policy and practice, I have always supported the local
church. Quite frankly, however, I have found that a lot of
churches are not worthy of that kind of support and confidence. Many congregations have become so self-centered and
introspective that they have little or no outward witness. They
do not preach the gospel; they show little or no interest in the
things that concern the heart of God. They place no emphasis
on training in discipleship and evangelism. Having lost their
first love, they are neither the "salt of the earth" nor the "light
of the world" (Matthew 5:13–14).

Our Lord said, "When the Holy Spirit has come upon you,
you will receive power to testify about me with great effect, to
the people in Jerusalem, throughout Judea, in Samaria, and to
the ends of the earth, about my death and resurrection" (Acts
1:8 TLB). The church that is not seeking to reach its Jerusalem
and extending its outreach to the uttermost parts of the earth
is disobedient to the Great Commission. Life is far too short
and dollars far too limited to try correcting a church or denom-
ination that is unfaithful to our Lord's command to disciple and
evangelize from our Jerusalem to the uttermost parts of the
earth.

In assessing our giving to the local church, we must ask
ourselves these questions: Is the holy, inspired Word of God

being proclaimed from the pulpit and in the community without compromise? Does the church have a world vision and an effective witnessing outreach into its own community? Is the church training disciples to help fulfill the Great Commission? If the local congregation is not walking in the power of the Holy Spirit, is not committed to its true biblical task, and is not willing to be influenced in this direction, it does not deserve our investment of time or money.

CHURCH STAFF

The Word of God also gives us the responsibility to meet the needs of those who minister the gospel. Meeting the needs of those who minister should be on a level "worthy of God" (3 John v. 6 NIV). Christian workers should be paid adequately to care for their needs. Forcing them to live in poverty or allowing them to enjoy the lap of luxury is not good stewardship. Providing for them in such a way that they have enough for their own needs and "plenty left over to give joyfully to others" (2 Corinthians 9:8 TLB) pleases God.

> *The cause of Christ is much bigger than a single congregation's outreach.*

WORLD MISSIONS

Giving to missions is a vital part of a steward's commitment as well. I would encourage every Christian to participate in the missions program of his church. However, a faithful steward should not channel his entire missions budget through the local body. The cause of Christ is much bigger than a single congregation's outreach. One should save a reasonable amount of whatever the Lord entrusts to him to help such groups as

The Navigators, InterVarsity, Young Life, Youth for Christ, Child Evangelism Fellowship, World Vision, Fellowship of Christian Athletes, Campus Crusade for Christ, various Bible societies, and others. An extension of the church, these ministries touch the lives of tens of millions around the world with the gospel of Christ.

When you give to missions, think of investing money where it will help introduce the largest number of people to Christ and build them in their faith so that they in turn will win and disciple others. Select groups worthy of trust; then give of your time, prayers, and financial resources to help them fulfill the Great Commission.

PRIORITY 4: SOCIETY

Putting God first in our finances involves yet another priority—helping nonbelievers see the life-changing power of Jesus Christ as a result of our involvement in society, and ministering to the physical needs of God's children.

HELPING NONBELIEVERS

As a faithful steward, one should be a constructive member of secular life. Caring for the poor, the orphans, and the widows; participating in the local PTA; and giving of our time, talent, and treasure to agencies concerned for the welfare of the community is a godly responsibility. It is possible for a Christian ministry to be so involved in its worldwide strategy that it neglects local opportunities for service.

I frequently remind our leadership, "We need to be active in different civic groups and community projects where we live because in so doing we show that we are good citizens, and we become 'salt' and 'light' for our Lord in these situations."

Although we should invest our primary funds in support of our local church and in evangelizing the world, we must not isolate ourselves from society in our evangelistic endeavors and thus become insensitive to its needs. Rather, as the apostle Paul admonishes, "While we have opportunity, let us do good to all people" (Galatians 6:10 NASB), thereby showing the love of Christ and opening the hearts of people to the gospel.

HELPING FELLOW BELIEVERS

Contributing to the physical needs of our brothers and sisters in Christ also brings glory to our Lord. Paul said, "Let us do good unto all men, especially unto them who are of the household of faith" (Galatians 6:10 KJV). Christians all around us are hurting for compassionate help in times of distress.

A few years ago, Larry and Gail became Christians. Excited about serving the Lord, they grew rapidly in their spiritual walk, joyfully putting God first in every area of their lives. Soon, however, the couple faced a serious problem that challenged their faith.

Larry farmed with his father. As he shared Christ with him, his father angrily gave Larry an ultimatum to either renounce his faith or lose his share of the farm machinery in their partnership. Gently but firmly, Larry went on serving God despite his father's opposition.

With the high price of machinery and labor, Larry knew he could never afford all he needed for the next spring's planting. He and Gail prayed about their situation and determined they would never go back on the commitment they had made to the Lord. Together, they informed Larry's father of their decision and then waited confidently to see what God would do.

The Christian farmers in the area united in prayer over

Larry's situation. When they saw that he was without the means to put in his crop, they worked out a plan to help him. They loaned him equipment and bought diesel fuel, seed, and other necessary items. They gave freely of their time and labor to help Larry do his spring work in spite of their own long workdays.

Larry's potatoes and sugar beets were planted on time, and the harvest that autumn was good. For three years, he received help from these farmers until he no longer needed assistance.

As a result, the small community in which Larry lived was changed. People took note of the love and care these Christian families had shown for each other. Many joined small group Bible studies, and some eventually accepted God's love and forgiveness in their lives. The care of these neighboring farmers also inspired other Christians in the community, encouraging them in their faith.

The sacrificial giving of these farmers showed that God was first in their lives. As His steward, have you put Him first in your finances? Are you setting priorities to accomplish that goal?

Our Lord said, "Blessed is that servant whom his master will find so doing when he comes" (Luke 12:43 NKJV). As we obey His command to faithful stewardship, we too will receive the commendation of the Master. What a joyous reunion that will be when He returns!

8

Giving for the Right Reasons

G ood stewardship involves more than merely knowing and applying the principles and priorities of giving. Motives are essential parts of the picture as well. They determine our reasons for giving. Built upon the right attitudes, our motives will generate the kind of giving that pleases God and brings glory to His name.

By scrutinizing our reasons for giving, we may find both wrong and right motives.

WRONG MOTIVES FOR GIVING

H ave you ever seen old boxcars standing idle, rusting on the railroad tracks? Once they were valuable components of the transportation system. When they were no longer needed, however, they were switched onto a sidetrack and abandoned to stand useless and empty.

Our giving can resemble those boxcars. Since our goal in stewardship is to put God first, we start with good intentions. We give faithfully. In addition to the local church budget, we contribute to missions and respond to the needs of the poor.

Somewhere along the line, however, wrong motives cloud our vision. Losing sight of the purpose of our stewardship, we become ineffective, unfruitful, and useless to our Lord.

In the book of Acts, Luke relates the example of Ananias and Sapphira. Many had laid gifts at the apostles' feet for the care of the needy. They brought all the proceeds from the sales of their lands and houses. Ananias and Sapphira also sold their property and handed their gift to the apostles. Wanting to look as generous as everyone else, yet keep a portion for themselves, they misrepresented their contribution as the full amount of the sale. "While it remained unsold, did it not remain your own? And after it was sold, was it not under your control?" Peter confronted. "Why is it that you have conceived this deed in your heart?

"You have not lied to men but to God" (Acts 5:4 NASB). Their deceit exposed, Ananias and Sapphira died at the apostles' feet.

Peter did not rebuke them for giving only a part of their profit, but for lying. Their untruthfulness and wrongful motives had made their gifts unacceptable to God.

We may masquerade our improper motives so skillfully that they take on the characteristics of sincerity, but we cannot hide these hollow, sinful purposes from the One who sees all. As we examine our motives, let us be aware of the subtle ways in which we, too, can misrepresent our giving.

> *Losing sight of the purpose of our stewardship, we become ineffective, unfruitful, and useless to our Lord.*

TO MANIPULATE GOD

In recent years a distorted view of stewardship has emerged in Christian circles. If you give, the theory suggests, God must repay you up to a hundred times the original gift. The assumption is that, since God's law of sowing and reaping is predictable, one can manipulate it like a bank account. Lifting Scriptures out of context to lend credibility to this concept, its proponents make it sound logical and convincing. However, this give-to-get hypothesis has disillusioned many Christians who have not experienced the abundance they expected.

Although God promises a return of up to a "hundredfold" to His faithful stewards, He cannot be bribed, manipulated, or blackmailed into it.

> *Although God promises a return of up to a "hundredfold" to His faithful stewards, He cannot be bribed, manipulated, or blackmailed into it.*

The apostle Paul asks, "Who could ever offer to the Lord enough to induce him to act?" (Romans 11:35 TLB). In God's economy, getting is the result, not the goal, of our giving.

TO FULFILL A WHIM

Christians donate millions of dollars every year to organizations that appeal to their heartstrings through emotions or high-pressure Madison Avenue tactics. Many worthy ministries, meanwhile, lack sufficient funds to operate because their appeal is not popular enough. Giving that rides on such an emotional roller coaster achieves no objectives and sets up a dangerous hit-and-miss pattern that displeases God.

A purposeful steward does not give emotionally but considers the need prayerfully and carefully. He does not let a whim dictate his actions but appropriates the wisdom and power of almighty God to achieve much for the kingdom.

TO RELIEVE GUILT

Guilt motivates people to do many things. Attempts to give their way into God's favor in order to hide their neglect of spiritual matters are common. But the dollar has buying power only in temporal matters. The currency of the kingdom is not cash but obedience. Giving out of guilt ultimately leads to feelings of frustration and failure because such stewardship does not please our heavenly Father. God is looking for stewards who, with a pure heart, apply His Word to their daily lives.

TO INCREASE SELF-WORTH

One of the misfortunes in the body of Christ today is the preoccupation with self. Volumes of books have been written and many sermons have been preached on the need for personal fulfillment and a better self-image.

A healthy self-concept is, of course, vital to one's effectiveness as a witness for Christ. The knowledge that God views us as holy and righteous and totally forgiven, that we are free from condemnation because of what Christ has done for us, should inspire us out of gratitude and as an act of obedience to share His love and forgiveness with everyone who will listen. The emphasis on self-glorification, however, has resulted in spiritual feebleness, leaving much of the body of Christ introspective and unproductive.

The desire for a sense of self-worth motivates the stewardship of many Christians, who believe their generosity makes them look good in God's sight and in the eyes of the church.

However, because the focus of such giving is on themselves, they live empty and fruitless lives.

Like sowing poor seed in unfertile soil, giving for the sake of feeling good about ourselves can never be productive.

TO ACHIEVE RECOGNITION

Another wrong motive for giving is recognition. Ananias and Sapphira tried to impress others with their liberality. They thought they could buy a reputation for being generous. The consequences of their deception, however, were severe. Not only did they lose their lives, but the Scriptures also record their infamy for all to see, generation after generation.

Recognition in itself is not wrong. I often acknowledge and express my gratitude to people for their giving—not to exalt them, but to encourage them to share their testimony with others. Giving for the sake of recognition, however, leaves a pathetic legacy.

TO GAIN POWER

The lust for power drives some to give. Churches and other Christian ministries often face the problem of a donor trying to control them with a sizable gift. A member of a church, for example, may give his pastor a new car or the down payment on a luxurious new home. The member may use his gift to gain a position of influence over the pastor and a favored status in the church.

Some donors try to buy their way into leadership. Acts 8:17–24 records how Simon offered money for spiritual power. As a sorcerer, he had enjoyed great influence and prestige because of what he could do. Simon gave up his sorcery to follow Christ, but he still had a thirst for power.

As Peter and John laid hands on the people to receive the Holy Spirit, Simon was envious.

"Let me have this power, too," he pleaded, "so that when I lay my hands on people, they will receive the Holy Spirit" (Acts 8:19).

The apostle Peter's response to such motivation applies equally today. "Your money perish with you for thinking God's gift can be bought!" he exclaimed. "You can have no part in this, for your heart is not right before God" (Acts 8:20–21).

To Gain Tax Advantages

The temptation of Christians in the higher income brackets is to regulate their giving for maximum tax advantage. Indeed, good stewardship requires that they avail themselves of every legal tax exemption available. Giving additional sums to God's work before the end of the year is sound financial planning. A true test of their motives and faithfulness in stewardship, however, is whether they would continue to give if the government were to drop deductions for religious and charitable giving.

The goal of giving, we have seen, is to put God first in our lives. If we give merely for the tax deduction, our motive is wrong. By focusing on our own gain, we rob God of His glory, and our giving is unfruitful.

Are your reasons for giving pleasing to the Lord Jesus? Our giving should be a natural expression of love and obedience to God. If you aren't giving joyfully, you're really missing out.

RIGHT MOTIVES FOR GIVING

The apostle Paul wrote: "Godliness actually is a means of great gain when accompanied by contentment. For we have brought nothing into the world, so we cannot take anything out of it either" (1 Timothy 6:6–7 NASB).

Godly motives produce eternal results. How we handle our money actively indicates our purpose—whether heavenly or earthly—in giving.

TO EXPRESS LOVE FOR GOD

We cannot find a more pure motive for giving than to express our love for God.

If we truly love the Lord Jesus, we will be sensitive to those who are close to His heart—the poor, the orphans, and the widows, and those who have not yet accepted the gift of God's Son.

A few years ago, Vonette and I decided that at Christmas time, instead of buying gifts for each other, we would give to someone who had a real need. Just before Christmas, we called several people who work in an inner-city ministry in San Bernardino, California, to ask if they knew of anyone who needed help. We learned about a woman whose husband had just left her with four children. A couple days later, we heard that the son of a former staff member had been killed in an accident, leaving his wife and children.

Helping these precious people was far more meaningful to us than placing presents for each other under our Christmas tree. We didn't give because we wanted spiritual "brownie points," nor were our hearts set on a heavenly reward. We gave because the love of God shed abroad in our hearts constrained us to reach out in compassion to them.

TO PLEASE GOD

A second reason for giving is to please God. The apostle Paul exhorts, "Our aim is to please him always in everything we do" (2 Corinthians 5:9 TLB). One Sunday morning an excited little girl gave her pastor $4.32 for missions. "How did you get so much money?" he asked, surprised.

"I earned it by collecting rainwater and selling it to the washerwomen who live on the edge of our town," she smiled proudly. "They paid me two cents a bucket! Now I want to send a missionary to tell boys and girls about Jesus."

The amazed pastor took the money and asked, "Shall I say, 'A gift from Mary'?"

"Oh, no!" Mary shook her head firmly. "I don't want *anyone* to know but Jesus. Put it down as rain from heaven."

TO LAY UP TREASURES IN HEAVEN

Many Christians miss the special blessing of God because they do not obey our Lord's command recorded in the gospel of Matthew:

> "Don't store up treasures here on earth where they can erode away or may be stolen. Store them in heaven where they will never lose their value, and are safe from thieves. If your profits are in heaven your heart will be there too."
>
> MATTHEW 6:19–21 TLB

Motivation is a key factor in accumulating heavenly wealth. Jesus knew that by storing up treasures on earth, we would soon take on the appearance of the world. Through selfish desires, we would cease to reflect the character of God and seek our own glory. By laying up treasures in heaven, on the other hand, we would declare the glory of His kingdom.

Everything we do to bring men and women into the kingdom of God, every act of kindness, every expression of love, is laying up treasure in God's storehouse. We must give out of love for God and our gratitude for His love and sacrifice through our Savior Jesus Christ. Having given with such love, what a joyous privilege it will be one day to lay our treasures before the feet of our wonderful Lord.

TO BE A CHANNEL OF BLESSING

God has given us the awesome privilege of channeling His abundant resources to a desperately needy world. As instruments to accomplish His will, we will never lack anything for the task. Dr. H. C. Morrison, a famous Holiness Methodist preacher, was walking along a busy street one day when he received five dollars from a stranger. "Thank you, friend," Dr. Morrison smiled as he resumed his walk. Soon he met a poor widow. Knowing her need, he gave her the money he had just received.

A few minutes later, as the preacher continued his walk, another stranger pressed another five dollars into his hand. Dr. Morrison soon met another needy person and felt strongly impressed to give the second five dollars to him. This time, however, Morrison decided to keep the money for himself.

"Strange to say, that was the last gift of five dollars I received that day," Dr. Morrison said. "I believe God would have continued the chain of money coming to me as I walked along if I had passed it on."

To Help Reach the World for Christ

There is no trouble too great, no humiliation too deep, no suffering too severe, no love too strong, no labor too hard, no expense too large if it is spent in the effort to win a soul.

As faithful stewards, our primary financial responsibility is to help worthy ministries reach the largest number of people for Christ possible.

Our Lord's last command before He ascended into heaven was, "Go therefore and make disciples of all the nations" (Matthew 28:19 NKJV).

How important are His final words to us as stewards of the things He has given us! Do we share God's priorities and His love for the lost? We can answer this question only by examining our hearts and our checkbooks—to see if our stewardship truly furthers His kingdom. Maintaining right motives through the power of the Holy Spirit is an urgent task if we are to accomplish this objective to the glory of God, and there can be no greater joy than being a part of that task.

9

The Blessing of the Tithe

One afternoon, Grandpa Clark arrived home, pockets bulging with treats for his grandchildren. As he settled into his creaking rocker, the children clamored around him with expectant faces.

The gray-haired man dug deep into his pockets and pulled out a fistful of candy, handing each child his or her favorite treat. When he finished, Grandpa leaned back with a smile of contentment to watch them tear at the wrappings.

On his left, two jealous brothers argued over whose flavor of hard candy tasted better. Another child sat at his feet, munching a candy bar. Suddenly, a tiny red-haired sweetheart patted her grandpa on the arm. Concern furrowed her brow.

"Would you like some of my M&M's, Grandpa?" she asked with sad, shy eyes. "You don't have anything."

Grandpa Clark peered down at his only granddaughter and grinned. Gently, he gathered her dainty form into his lap. "Why, you haven't even opened your candy," he observed.

She stared into his eyes with a frank expression. "'Cause I want you to have the first one."

"Why, thank you, I think I will," he smiled, carefully tearing open her little package. With relish, he removed a couple of colored candies and popped them into his mouth. Then he wrapped his arms tightly around her, engulfing her happy face. Both of them beamed.

This story brightly illustrates tithing—giving back to God the first part of what He has given to us.

THE BLESSING OF THE TITHE

The word *tithe* itself comes from an Old English term simply meaning a tenth. However, Christian leaders use tithe in two different senses. To some, tithe means the general

❖

Systematic, purposeful giving ensures consistent stewardship.

giving of a tenth of one's income or resources to God. To others, tithe refers to the specific manner of funding God's work mandated by Mosaic law. I use tithe in the first sense. Tithing is important in every Christian's life for several reasons.

IT'S A GUIDELINE FOR SYSTEMATIC GIVING
(1 CORINTHIANS 16:2)

Systematic, purposeful giving ensures consistent steward-ship. Without a functional plan, we fall prey to our whims. One day we feel excited about giving; the next we may forget. Even worse, we may not feel like giving at all. A practical plan for giving, however, enables us to circumvent the emotions and circumstances that would hinder us from being faithful stewards.

IT'S A RELEASE FROM MATERIAL TYRANNY
(MALACHI 3:10)

Spiritual blessings are incomparably superior to material ones. When a steward gives the first portion of his income to God, he receives an abundance of joy and peace. When we hang on to our possessions, they own us. Tithing releases us from the tyranny of materialism and clears the channel for God's abundant blessings.

IT ACKNOWLEDGES GOD AS THE SOURCE
(PSALM 24:1)

Tithing performs a role opposite that of mere giving, which suggests that we own all that we possess. As stewards of what God entrusts to us, we set aside a portion to use for the cause of Christ.

When we give out of our own generosity, on the other hand, we take the credit for ourselves. We imply that the responsibility for the gift lies with our own efforts. We donate to this person or that one and to this cause or that. A selfish spirit infects our giving, and we impress others that we are the masters of our faith and of our possessions. Only those who tithe in the biblical way truly glorify God with their gifts.

Christians should view tithing as a voluntary act of worship (1 Chronicles 16:29; Psalm 29:2). Through this act, we keep our focus on the heavenly Father and testify to His kindness and generosity toward us.

IT TEACHES US TO PUT GOD FIRST
(PROVERBS 3:9)

How often have we conceived grand strategies for giving, only to find that the money we intended to give vanished in day-to-day spending? Covetousness, greed, and frivolous buying all tempt even the most dedicated Christian. When budgets stretch unmanageably or a crisis depletes the paycheck, many Christians skimp on their tithe to cover a personal deficit.

Giving 10 percent to God's work is a realistic starting point for a steward who wants to honor and glorify God with all of his or her resources. In addition, by giving 10 percent to God's work, we exhibit our priorities and show our trust that God will provide all our needs.

TITHING TIME AND TALENT

The blessing of tithing also applies to the use of our time and talents. Are we giving them to God as we give our money to Him? Do we give Him our best time or what's left over after a busy day? Do we give Him the same talents that we give to our professional endeavors? Remember, your time and your talent are not yours any more than your money is yours. God has given all these things to you to be used for His purposes.

A faithful steward serves because he has a heart for God. He labors lovingly, gratefully, and obediently, knowing that nothing he can ever do will compare with what God has done for him.

Do we give Him our best time or what's left over after a busy day?

Everything we have is a gift from God. Every second of every minute, every minute of every hour, twenty-four hours a day, belong to Him. He gives us our abilities and the strength and wisdom to use them, and He holds us accountable for the way we manage these precious gifts.

The stewardship of our time and talents must not stop with the mere doing. Whether teaching a Sunday school class or taking a meal to an elderly shut-in, all we do must flow from a heart filled with praise and worship. Dedicating ourselves to the work of the Lord in this manner pleases Him and opens the channels of His blessing in our lives.

So in addition to tithing financially, I challenge you to give a tithe of your day, week, or month to the Lord. You will be amazed at how much more you will accomplish in the remaining nine-tenths. Results will show in various ways. God may help you increase your efficiency. Others may offer to help you with a time-consuming project. The demands on your time may lessen. Ask God to show you how to use your talents and time for His glory.

God is generous to every servant who sincerely places Him first. He will give back to us many times over everything we offer to Him out of gratitude and love.

―――――――― ❖ ――――――――

"I HAVE LEARNED, IN WHATSOEVER STATE I AM,
THEREWITH TO BE CONTENT."

PHILIPPIANS 4:11 KJV

―――――――――――――――――

10

God Wants You
to Be Financially Free

In July 1903, a young man moved to Chicago intent on making his fortune. With only a few years of experience working with dairy products, he decided to set his theories about cheese making into operation.

Starting his enterprise with only $65 in his pocket, a cart, and a rented horse named Paddy, he worked hard selling cheese direct to Chicago retailers. By the end of the first year, he was $3,000 in debt. Soon, no one would give him credit to run his business.

He worked harder. Still, success eluded him. Finally, one day he loaded his wagon determined to sell more than $100 worth of cheese. When he counted the money from his sales at the end of the day, however, he had taken in only $12.65. He turned Paddy toward home, dazed and beaten.

"Paddy, what's the matter with us anyhow?" he asked dejectedly.

Paddy's ears laid back, and out of the air the young man seemed to hear the answer: "You are working without God!" He stopped the horse and looked around but saw no one. As he sat wondering, he realized that he had left God out of his business. Right there, he determined to make Him a partner.

The man who made this momentous decision was J. L. Kraft, founder of what is now Kraft Foods Inc. The Lord blessed his commitment, and within a few years the company owned more than fifty subsidiaries with operations in Canada, Australia, England, and Germany. Today, Kraft is a household word in dairy products.

> *As men and women have proved faithful, He has made them channels of love and blessing.*

I met Mr. Kraft, a humble, godly man, in the 1940s at a meeting for businessmen. His example of stewardship is a model for us all. He began tithing when he earned barely $20 a week and continued investing in God's work throughout his life. Sometimes he donated more than one-third of his income to the cause of Christ.

Mr. Kraft achieved financial freedom through wise business practices and by applying biblical stewardship principles. He not only supported his church, but also helped further religious education. He also gave liberally to home and foreign missions.

Although God has blessed many of His children with wealth, most of us can only dream about financial independence. Financial freedom, however, is available to every Christian steward who faithfully follows God's plan for giving, saving, and spending.

FINANCIAL FREEDOM

Financial freedom means having enough to provide adequately for our households and to give generously and joyfully to God's work. From the beginning, this has been God's plan. He has prospered those who have demonstrated good stewardship and showed themselves worthy of trust in spiritual as well as material things (Luke 12:42; 16:10–11). As men and women have proved faithful, He has made them channels of love and blessing.

God wants us to be financially free so we can put Him first in our life and give liberally to the advancement of His kingdom. He wants us to be sensitive to His voice, ready to follow Him whenever—and wherever—He leads. This is a difficult task when one is under constant financial pressure!

Whether or not we are willing to admit it, money worries drain us emotionally and spiritually. They rob us of creative energy. They steal our peace of mind and keep us from being fruitful disciples for our Lord. The average Christian, burdened with

> *Whether or not we are willing to admit it, money worries drain us emotionally and spiritually.*

payments and expenses, cannot give with joy and thanksgiving as God desires. Deaf to the voice of God, he does not hear when our Lord calls and does not see where He leads in his finances. Countless millions of dollars have been lost for the cause of Christ and His kingdom in this manner because unfaithful stewards have diverted funds for selfish fulfillment.

If this is not God's plan, why do many Christians live in financial bondage? The reasons are basic. Not understanding or obeying scriptural principles of stewardship, these Christians succumb to the world's philosophy of money. They shackle themselves with materialism and make little or no commitment to God's work.

INSATIABLE APPETITES

Malcolm Muggeridge, one of England's leading intellectuals, came to our Christian Embassy headquarters in Washington, D.C., for lunch one day. We talked about the things of God. On that day, he offered little hope for the future of the Western world.

The love of money and the love of things are slowly destroying the average person in America and in Western Europe, he explained. People are greedy, grasping for more than they have. Our appetites know no bounds; we have become insatiable.

As a result, he said, there is more vital Christianity in Eastern Germany than in Western Germany, in Poland than in Italy, in the Soviet Union than in England. The Christians who willingly have paid the price of persecution in these countries have learned to seek first the kingdom of God and His righteousness and to be satisfied with what they have. With humility of heart, they join the apostle Paul in saying, "I have learned, in whatsoever state I am, therewith to be content" (Philippians 4:11 KJV).

It is in the faithful stewardship of that which God entrusts to us, not materialism, that we find fulfillment and true meaning to life.

First and foundational, since Christ's church is like a body, every member must surrender to the Head. Christ must be Lord of all areas of our being. The effective members in the body of Christ have made total, irrevocable commitments of their lives—including their finances—to the Lord Jesus. The ineffective members live as slaves to their greed, wrong attitudes, and improper priorities.

Lacking commitment to God's work, they fail to give consistently, if at all.

To escape from the bondage of materialism, they must deal with the sin of selfishness.

As faithful stewards, we will become world Christians. Nothing pleases the heart of God more than seeing His children involved in helping to fulfill the Great Commission by faithfully giving of their finances, prayers, and, yes, even their lives.

MYTHS ABOUT MONEY

Wrong assumptions about money also contribute to financial bondage. Some Christians find virtue in poverty. Others measure success by capital assets and net worth. Whether poor or rich, they are slaves to mammon. What are these destructive assumptions?

MYTH: MONEY IS THE ROOT OF ALL EVIL

Money itself is not the root of evil; however, "the *love* of money is a root of all kinds of evil, for which some have strayed from the faith in their greediness, and pierced themselves through with many sorrows" (1 Timothy 6:10 NKJV). Money is simply a medium of exchange. From God's perspective, only one's devotion to riches causes him or her grief.

MYTH: TO HAVE MONEY IS SIN

I do not believe that, as Christians, we should concern ourselves with how large our bank account is, or how big our home should be, or how prestigious our cars can look. Instead, our focus must be on how we manage the resources God has given us to invest for the cause of Christ. There is nothing wrong, however, with bank accounts, beautiful homes, or nice cars. If every Christian lived in poverty, nonbelievers would not listen to what we have to say.

Many men of the Bible were wealthy: for example, Abraham, Job, and Solomon. The Scriptures teach that "in the house of the righteous there is much treasure" (Proverbs 15:6 NKJV) and "as for every man to whom God has given riches and wealth, and given him power to eat of it, to receive his heritage and rejoice in his labor—this is the gift of God" (Ecclesiastes 5:19 NKJV).

Today, God has blessed multitudes of committed Christians with wealth, which they use to support the church and help organizations win and disciple millions around the world for His kingdom.

The Holy Spirit used people of means to draw me to Jesus Christ. As a materialistic, young nonbeliever, a happy pagan, I depended upon my own abilities. I had never met a Christian businessman whom I admired. When I moved to Hollywood, however, I suddenly found myself face-to-face with some of the most prominent Christian business and professional leaders in Los Angeles.

Although some of my newly found friends were wealthy, they did not attribute happiness to their lovely cars and beautiful estates. They lived for Jesus Christ only, and that gave me a whole new perspective on Christianity. I became receptive to the gospel because I met Christians who were successful. They taught me that one does not have to live in a dump or drive a jalopy to be a Christian.

Whether wealthy or of humble means, we need the right perspective. Since everything belongs to God, what we have is not important; only what possesses us counts. True prosperity means having enough resources to accomplish what God calls us to do.

Myth: One Must Be Poor to Be Spiritual

One's financial status does not necessarily reflect that person's spirituality. The apostle Paul is an example. He said, "I know how to be abased, and I know how to abound" (Philippians 4:12 NKJV). In Paul's lifetime, he experienced both poverty and riches. He knew what it meant to go hungry and to suffer need. He also enjoyed the blessings of abundance. Through it all, he wrote, "I have learned the secret of contentment in every situation" (Philippians 4:12 TLB). This is the key to spirituality.

Some of the most godly people I know are among the most wealthy. Although worth millions, they are filled with the Holy Spirit and walk in the joy and wonder of our Lord's resurrection.

A poor person not committed to the Lord Jesus can be as guilty of wrongful motives and unbiblical attitudes as a wealthy one. Virtue is not inherent in poverty or riches. Our life does not consist in the abundance—or lack—of the things we possess (Luke 12:15 NKJV). God desires that we have enough resources to meet our needs and to carry out His will. Balance is the key. "Give me neither poverty nor riches," God's Word says. "Feed me with the food allotted to me; lest I be full and deny You, and say, 'Who is the LORD?' Or lest I be poor and steal, and profane the name of my God" (Proverbs 30:8–9 NKJV).

Myth: Money Provides Security

From the time of our birth, we have an instinctive desire to feel safe. Throughout our lives, we strive for strength, pursue

n, and concentrate on certainty. The lure of money
s these innate desires.

Money is deceptive, temporary, and corruptive. Bible verse
after Bible verse bears this out. In His parable of the sower, our
Lord explained that the "deceitfulness of riches" chokes the
Word and makes it unfruitful in our hearts (Mark 4:19 NKJV).
Solomon observed, "When goods increase, they increase who

> *Earthly riches never
> fully satisfy the heart.*

eat them; so what profit have the
owners except to see them with their
eyes? The sleep of a laboring man is
sweet, whether he eats little or much;
but the abundance of the rich will not
permit him to sleep" (Ecclesiastes 5:11–12 NKJV). "Riches are
not forever," the writer of Proverbs records (27:24 NKJV). Our
Lord warned, "Do not lay up for yourselves treasures on earth,
where moth and rust destroy and where thieves break in and
steal" (Matthew 6:19 NKJV). The apostle Paul cautioned Timothy,
"People who long to be rich soon begin to do … things that hurt
them and make them evil-minded and finally send them to hell
itself" (1 Timothy 6:9 TLB).

MYTH: MONEY BRINGS HAPPINESS

If money truly brings happiness, some in the world would
have cause for jubilation.

Wealth cannot guarantee happiness. Earthly riches never
fully satisfy the heart. Rather, happiness stems from a vital
relationship with God. I have discovered that individuals of
modest means who love God generally experience the most
contentment.

Throughout the ages, Satan has schemed to distort, to
enslave, and to destroy. When God said "Love," Satan said

"Hate." When our Lord said "Have faith," the Devil said "Seeing is believing." When Jesus said "Give," Satan said "Get."

The Devil's tactics for leading Christians into financial bondage are varied and treacherous. Appealing to our senses, he emphasizes getting instead of giving, covetousness over contentment, greed rather than need, and fear in place of faith.

❖

God intended for material blessings to enable us to serve Him more freely and more fully.

God intended for material blessings to enable us to serve Him more freely and more fully. Satan knows the key to these blessings is giving. He aims to keep us from it, and thereby make us ineffective in our service to God.

I encourage you to obey God's Word, proving yourself a good steward worthy of His trust. Be sensitive to His voice, and be ready to follow Him wherever He leads. Enjoy the adventurous life of faith—a "faith that will not shrink, though pressed by every foe, a faith that shines more bright and clear when tempests rage without; that when in danger knows no fear, and in darkness feels no doubt."[1]

---

1. Lois Neely, *Fire in His Bones: The Official Biography of Oswald J. Smith* (Wheaton, Ill.: Tyndale House Publishers, 1982) pp. 232–233.

IT TAKES BOTH THE WIDOW'S MITE AND THE WEALTHY
MAN'S ABUNDANCE TO ACCOMPLISH THE WORK OF GOD.

11

How to Be Financially Free

If someone offered you the opportunity to become financially free, would you take it? I would guess your answer is "yes." However, did you know the Lord offers you this chance—right now—in His Word?

Let me share with you specific steps you can take to guarantee financial freedom for you and your family.

God's will about money is not a mystery. Biblical principles of stewardship give us a clear revelation of His plan. By basing our decisions on these precepts, we will experience lasting financial freedom.

KNOW AND OBEY GOD'S WILL FOR YOUR LIFE

Every investment of time, talent, and treasure, unless otherwise directed by the Holy Spirit, should be determined by the sound-mind principle of Scripture recorded in 2 Timothy 1:7: "God has not given us a spirit of fear, but of power and of love and of a sound mind" (NKJV).

Additionally, we should seek the wise counsel of godly, successful people.

There are times in each of our lives, however, when difficult situations will arise for which no scriptural principle or human counsel offers specific direction. We wonder which to take and how to know for sure if our decisions are right. Even then God makes provision for guidance.

The apostle Paul instructs, "Let the peace of Christ rule in your hearts, since as members of one body you were called to peace" (Colossians 3:15 NIV). What does this mean?

Peace is a gift and a calling. The Holy Spirit guides us by His presence or His absence in our hearts. When we make the right decisions, we will sense incredible calm even in circumstances that seem impossible. When our actions do not coincide with His plan, however, we will feel restless, perhaps even churn inside.

No better way exists for us to know God's will in our financial decisions than to base our actions on the principles of His Word and then to invite the peace of God to guide us from within.

BREATHE SPIRITUALLY

Spiritual Breathing is the secret to living the Spirit-filled life from moment to moment. In Spiritual Breathing we "exhale" the impurities of sin by confession. Then we "inhale" the purity of righteousness by appropriating the fullness of God's Spirit by faith as an act of the will, inviting Him to direct, control, and empower our life.

Good stewardship is a call to supernatural living. No matter how financially wise we may be, we will succumb to material bondage and fruitlessness unless the Holy Spirit controls our life. Unconfessed sin dams the channel of God's blessing. Maintaining short accounts with God through Spiritual Breathing unclogs the flow.

BREATHE FINANCIALLY!

As Spiritual Breathing sustains our spiritual health, so "financial breathing" preserves our financial freedom.

We exhale finan-
cially by relinquishing
the ownership of our
resources to God, by
surrendering every deci-

This simple act of faith calls for a total, irrevocable commitment to God's ownership over our lives.

sion to Him and accepting His direction, and by acknowledging His lordship over all our time, talents, and treasure.

We inhale financially by sharing with others the abundance God provides.

This simple act of faith calls for a total, irrevocable commitment to God's ownership over our lives.

GIVE GENEROUSLY

God does not require us to give because He needs the money. Rather, He chose giving as a method for securing our financial future.

Our Lord said, "If you will give, you will get! Your gift will return to you in full and overflowing measure, pressed down, shaken together to make room for more, and running over. Whatever measure you use to give—large or small—will be used to measure what is given back to you" (Luke 6:38 TLB).

Our Lord instructs us to give according to how He blesses us. If He gives us much, we are accountable for much; if He gives us little, we joyfully manage on little. Giving generously or sacrificially beyond our tithe truly honors our Lord.

DEVELOP A FINANCIAL PLAN

Built upon the foundation of biblical stewardship, financial goals provide the framework for our economic decisions. All Christians do not agree on this issue. Some argue that planning keeps us from relying on God. Others create such rigid plans that they cannot respond to His leading.

Balanced planning reflects the nature of God. The very structure of the universe depends on the intricate order of its elements. If one particle within an atom were to stray from its path around the nucleus, for example, chaos would result. Living without a financial plan also will produce disaster.

A written financial plan gives us a visible target. If prepared according to biblical standards of stewardship, the plan will enable us to measure our progress and stay on track.

BUDGET FAITHFULLY

Developing a financial plan is not difficult. The family budget serves as a starting point. Easily identifying our needs, wants, and desires, the plan provides a vehicle for setting priorities and forming strategic short-range and long-range goals. Furthermore, the budget enables us to think before we buy, thus keeping our spending on target.

The blessings of giving do not give license for foolish spending. God will not protect us from the consequences of irresponsible spending just because we tithe. He expects us to live within our means and to be content with what He provides.

MASTER YOUR CREDIT

Good stewardship requires that we live modestly and effectively manage credit.

Paul admonished, "Pay all your debts except the debt of love for others" (Romans 13:8 TLB). Many Christian leaders believe that one should never go in debt for anything. I disagree. A young couple will frequently incur monthly obligations while establishing their home. Throughout life, the purchase of large-dollar items—such as a house or a car— usually requires indebtedness. The real danger does not lie in the provision of needs, but in self-indulgence, poor planning, lack of discipline, and the passion to satisfy one's greed.

A faithful steward will never obligate himself to the place where he cannot, through control of his income, make a reasonable payout.

Give the first 10 percent of your income to God and save the second 10 percent for the surplus. Then live on the remaining 80 percent.

CREATE A SURPLUS

Surpluses seldom just happen: We must create them. Let me suggest a simple formula to accomplish this goal: Give the first 10 percent of your income to God and save the second 10 percent for the surplus. Then live on the remaining 80 percent.

These percentages may not be possible for everyone. With expenses gobbling up all their income, many Christians will find it difficult to save. Creating a surplus demands discipline and a change in spending habits.

You may adjust the amounts for savings and living expenses up or down to suit your needs, but whatever percentage you choose, saving to create a surplus will require sacrifice.

Financial emergencies usually hit us when we least expect them. Sometimes a crisis deals a devastating blow. God wants us to use part of His resources for our families.

Even so, the intent of His provision goes beyond our own needs. Paul captured the reason for the surplus with these words: "God is able to make it up to you by giving you everything you need and more, so that there will not only be enough for your own needs, but *plenty left over to give joyfully to others*" (2 Corinthians 9:8 TLB).

INVEST IN GOD'S KINGDOM

Every Christian should consider how to give in order to help win and disciple the largest possible number of people for Christ. If every child of God would do so—whether sacrificially or out of planned abundance—vast sums of money would be available to accelerate the fulfilling of the Great Commission, and the world as you know it would be dramatically changed.

I would rather place my confidence in the bank of heaven than in all the combined financial institutions of the world.

I would rather place my confidence in the bank of heaven than in all the combined financial institutions of the world. No investment—however large or small—pays greater dividends than what we deposit in the treasury of the heavenly kingdom.

Perhaps you are wondering, "How can I invest in the kingdom of God? I have no money, just my weekly paycheck, and I must pay rent, buy food and clothing, and take care of many other expenses." By putting God first in your life and applying the principles of stewardship that I have shared with you, you will be able to give. You have God's promise on that.

"But how much should I invest?" you ask. The amount will

not be the same for everyone. It takes both the widow's mite and the wealthy man's abundance to accomplish the work of God. Simply give until you feel satisfied that all the needs He has placed on your heart are met. I encourage you to ask Him to supply the funds to invest in His work. Look for a special project that you can support monthly, if only modestly, in addition to your commitment to your local church. Prayerfully make a faith-promise commitment that is more than you are capable of fulfilling according to your present income. Then expect God to honor this expression of your faith in Him and your obedience to His command to help fulfill the Great Commission.

—❖—

IF YOU OBEY THE LORD IN YOUR STEWARDSHIP,
"YOUR GIFT WILL RETURN TO YOU IN FULL
AND OVERFLOWING MEASURE."

LUKE 6:38 TLB

12

How to Trust God with Your Finances

Many of you reading this book make good incomes. In comparison to most of the world, the average westerner, especially the average American, would be considered wealthy. We own comfortable homes, two or more cars, nice clothes, and many of life's other blessings. Providing adequately for our spouses, children, and grandchildren is good stewardship. One does not live prudently in this world without a reasonable amount of insurance to cover medical needs, funeral expenses, and provision for those we leave behind. A good financial plan also will include preparation for retirement.

Some Christians do not stop there, however. Many spend a lifetime building financial security. Having plenty to live comfortably, they continue to accumulate more and more wealth. They hold on to their possessions and trap themselves in a lifestyle of overaccumulation.

Like any of our talents, the ability to make money is God given. In Deuteronomy, God's Word admonishes, "Always remember that it is the LORD your God who gives you power to become rich" (8:18). God gives us the ability to gain wealth, not to hoard but to share. Since the talent for making money belongs to God, He holds us accountable for what we do with it. Many neglect their responsibility as stewards and indulge themselves in overaccumulation.

Most people trust in their investments, savings, and retirement plans to ensure security and happiness—only to find their hopes dashed when reverses deplete their assets. Others accumulate sizable portfolios, then worry over their wealth. Many more plunge deeply into debt through unwise investments or uncontrolled spending. All are wasting their lives trying to achieve security in a volatile world.

Our heavenly Father, on the other hand, wants us to enjoy a full, abundant life free from the cares and stresses that relying on money brings. Rather than trusting in a worldly system that cannot assure our welfare, or trusting in our own weak capabilities to provide for our needs, He calls us to depend entirely on Him. That's the only true security we can ever have. Good stewardship requires trusting God with your finances. Let me suggest some essential steps you can take to develop that trust.

RECOGNIZE GOD IS WORTHY OF YOUR TRUST

We cannot separate God from His character. He is perfect in truth. The psalmist wrote, "The Lord's promise is sure. He speaks no careless word; all he says is purest truth, like silver seven times refined" (Psalm 12:6 TLB). We can count on God to do as He says because the One who created the heavens and earth and who set the laws that govern the universe is more capable of providing for our needs than we could ever imagine. Make Him the foundation of your financial security.

REALIZE GOD WANTS YOU TO LIVE AN ABUNDANT LIFE

Our Lord promises to give every obedient Christian an overflowing, joyous life, regardless of his financial position. Jesus told His followers, "I came that they may have life, and have it abundantly" (John 10:10 NASB). This generous assurance includes financial freedom.

KEEP YOUR HEART AND MOTIVES PURE

Having trust in God by itself will not enable us to live abundantly. Any number of impure incentives may divert our aim to put God first in our stewardship. I encourage you to breathe spiritually when motives displeasing to our Lord creep into your heart. Confess these wrongful attitudes; then appropriate the Holy Spirit to help you rely on Him to supply your needs.

SUBSTITUTE FAITH FOR FEAR

One emotion that can undermine our faith and throw us back into financial bondage is fear. When anxiety over the future grips us, we lose the ability to trust God for our needs.

Faith is our defense against fear. It is like an anchor cast into the sea of God's mercy to keep us from sinking into the despair of doubt.

By obeying God's will for our lives, we substitute faith for our fear. When we actively do His commands, we establish our faith firmly and open our lives to His abundant blessings. Our Lord promises in John 14:21, "The one who obeys me is the one who loves me; and because he loves me, my Father will love him; and I will too, and I will reveal myself to him" (TLB).

ASK GOD TO SUPPLY YOUR NEEDS

The apostle James observed, "You do not have because you do not ask" (James 4:2 NKJV). Faith requires action. Ask God, as an act of your will, to supply your needs. Do not allow emotions or circumstances to hinder your requests.

There is unlimited power in the name of Jesus to whom God has given all authority in heaven and on earth. God wants us to ask Him for everything, in Jesus' name. Matthew writes, "You can get anything—*anything* you ask for in prayer—if you believe" (21:22 TLB). I encourage you to trust your heavenly Father as the source of all things and to relax in the certainty that He will fulfill His promises.

TAKE A STEP OF FAITH

Dr. Oswald J. Smith had a passion "to bring back the King through world evangelization." The entire ministry of his People's Church in Toronto centered on this vision. The high point of each year was the four-week Annual Missionary Convention. To Dr. Smith, raising support for missions was the prime duty of every individual.

Each year, he would challenge them to decide on a "faith promise," which they felt God would put into their hands to give to missions above their regular giving—even if they could not see a way in their budget. No one received a reminder, and miraculously, each year more than the amount promised came in.[1]

A faith promise involves three key principles. First, it is

an agreement between us and God. No one will try to collect. Second, it is a commitment, not a pledge. (Pledges are made on the basis of what we can give out of our own resources.) Third, it is a plan for giving that enables every Christian to have a part in helping to fulfill the Great Commission.

Taking such a step of faith enriches our life beyond measure. It enables us to venture beyond safe boundaries into new territory. It encourages us to believe God for the impossible.

As your faith in God and His love and trustworthiness grows, let me encourage you to prayerfully make a faith promise—one that is greater than you are capable of fulfilling according to your present income. Take God at His word to supply from His unlimited resources, and make a generous faith promise to help fulfill the Great Commission.

Then, expect a miracle! God has promised in His Word: "Call to Me, and I will answer you, and show you great and mighty things, which you do not know" (Jeremiah 33:3 NKJV). With our faith and trust, we link our finite lives with the infinite God, the God of love, power, wisdom, and sufficiency. We tie ourselves into His inexhaustible supply of answered prayer. We become His instruments for changing the world.

KEEP YOUR FAITH ACTIVE

At some time in our lives, each of us must give by faith. When we exhaust our resources, God may open an opportunity for us to invest in a worthwhile cause, or He may show us an individual in need.

What, then, shall we do? Remember God's faithfulness and trustworthiness. On that basis, release your faith and keep on giving. Our Lord will never remain in your debt. If you obey the Lord in your stewardship, "your gift will return to you in full and overflowing measure" (Luke 6:38 TLB), and you will live a joyous, abundant life.

---

1. 2 Corinthians 9:7, *Letters to Young Churches: A Translation of the New Testament Epistles* by J. B. Phillips (New York: The Macmillian Company, 1957).

13

Live It!

A father and his two teenage sons prepared for a month-long camping trip in the mountains. They had packed their equipment and drawn their map. On the morning they were to leave, each dressed in hiking clothes with a sense of excitement.

Ready for their big adventure, the boys gathered their gear and hurried out the door. "Boys! Come back here and sit down for a minute," their father called. "There's one more item we need before we start."

The boys looked at each other and groaned. "Oh, Dad!" the older one exclaimed. "We've gone over our plans and equipment several times to make sure we haven't forgotten anything."

"Yes, you've been very thorough," the father agreed. "But what I'm talking about will determine whether our trip will be a magnificent experience or a huge disaster."

"Tell me what it is and I'll go buy one," the younger son joked.

His father laughed, then sobered. "We can't buy it at any

price. There'll be times during our trip when you will want to turn back. You'll feel so tired you can barely plant one foot in front of the other. You may have to sleep cold and wet. Our food supply may run low.

> *We, too, are about to begin an adventure—the adventure of giving by faith.*

"Each of us must firmly resolve to put every ounce of his strength to last through the month. If we commit all our strength, will, and wisdom to what lies ahead, this trip will be the most thrilling expedition we ever take together. Are you ready to commit?"

The boys nodded enthusiastically. "We're willing and ready!"

"Let's go, then!" the father exclaimed, shouldering his pack.

We, too, are about to begin an adventure—the adventure of giving by faith. We have equipped ourselves with the biblical principles of giving. We have charted our course by God's Word. Let us now commit to applying these precepts in faithful stewardship.

The joyful and abundant life that our Lord promises to His faithful stewards never ends, for He continually finds creative ways in which to bless us. I am always amazed at the miraculous ways He uses us to help others as we put Him first in our finances.

God reserves a special blessing for those who give generously of their time, talents, and treasure to His work. Have you made your commitment to support your church and help fulfill the Great Commission through faithful stewardship?

I urge you to develop a personal strategy for giving that will enable you to invest wisely in the kingdom of God and increase your effectiveness for Christ. Acknowledge God as the source and owner of your possessions, and be ready to give an account of your stewardship to Him. Offer your gifts to the Lord Jesus as an act of praise and worship. Put God first in your giving. And manage your time, talents, and treasure to bring glory to His name. In so doing, you, too, will experience the wonderful adventure of living and giving by faith.

Readers' Guide

For Personal Reflection or Group Discussion

Questions are an inevitable part of life. Proud parents ask their new baby, "Can you smile?" Later they ask, "Can you say 'Mama'?" "Can you walk to Daddy?" The early school years bring the inevitable, "What did you learn at school today?" Later school years introduce tougher questions, "If X equals 12 and Y equals −14, then …?" Adulthood adds a whole new set of questions. "Should I remain single or marry?" "How did things go at the office?" "Did you get a raise?" "Should we let Susie start dating?" "Which college is right for Kyle?" "How can we possibly afford to send our kids to college?"

This book raises questions, too. The following study guide is designed to (1) maximize the subject material and (2) apply biblical truth to daily life. You won't be asked to solve any algebraic problems or recall dates associated with obscure events in history, so relax. Questions asking for objective information are based solely on the text. Most questions, however, prompt you to search inside your soul, examine the circumstances that surround your life, and decide how you can best use the truths communicated in the book.

Honest answers to real issues can strengthen your faith, draw you closer to the Lord, and lead you into fuller, richer, more joyful, and productive daily adventures. So confront each question head-on and expect the One who is the answer for all of life's questions and needs to accomplish great things in your life.

Chapter 1: The Adventure of Giving

1. How is the word *steward* used in the New Testament?

2. List categories of items over which God has made you a steward. How does the concept of stewardship change your perspective about what you "own"?

3. The author indicates that most of what a Christian gives to God's work should be related to the fulfilling of the Great Commission. Why do you agree or disagree with the author's conviction?

4. How can a believer make the act of giving an adventure?

5. Why is faithful stewardship essential to walking in the Spirit's fullness and power?

Chapter 2: Qualifications of a Steward

1. What attitude should a faithful steward adopt if he experiences financial loss?

2. What qualities of stewardship does the author cite? Which of these qualities are most prominent in your stewardship? Which ones do you need to strengthen?

3. What guidelines should a believer follow when selecting ministries worthy of financial support?

4. How is godly living related to stewardship?

5. Do you think God wants our money if we lead an unholy life? Why or why not?

Chapter 3: Attitudes of a Steward

1. Should Christians give to God's work only when they feel like doing so? Defend your answer.

2. Do you agree or disagree that it is unwise to give generously to the Lord's work in a time of personal financial crisis? Defend your answer.

3. How does a person become a "hilarious giver"?

4. The author cites examples of hilarious giving. What examples have you observed?

5. How might an increase in hilarious giving benefit your church?

Chapter 4: Responsibilities of a Steward

1. Which of the nine attributes of God listed by the author motivates you most to give to God's work? Why?

2. Knowing that God is sovereign and self-sufficient, what might be His reasons for encouraging us to give to Him?

3. How might a Christian restructure his time in order to be a better steward?

4. What do you see as the difference between a spiritual gift and a natural talent? How might a good steward use both to help fulfill the Great Commission?

5. What opportunities do you believe your church has to reach nonbelievers for Christ? What opportunities do you have?

CHAPTER 5: WHY GIVING MAKES SENSE

1. How would you respond to someone who suggests that it is unspiritual to talk about giving?

2. What examples of giving do you recall from Jesus' life and ministry?

3. Why is it wrong to give to God in order to get a good return for our investment?

4. Why do you agree or disagree that a stingy Christian cannot possess a vibrant faith?

5. How might a Christian's generosity open a recipient's heart to God's love and forgiveness? If you have witnessed this phenomenon, describe briefly what occurred.

CHAPTER 6: THE LAW OF THE HARVEST

1. What does it mean to sow righteously?

2. How can believers determine the quality of soil before they plant financial seeds?

3. What does it mean to die to self? Generally speaking, what selfish desires would cease to exist if Christians died to self?

4. How can a hobby or even a close friend become an idol?

5. What fruit would you like to see your giving produce?

CHAPTER 7: THE GOAL OF GIVING

1. What biblical order of priority does the Bible assign to society, God, family, and church?

2. What relationship, if any, do you see between loving God and obeying the Great Commission?

3. How do you explain the high rate of divorce among Christians? What, if anything, does it have to do with biblical priorities?

4. How can parents show their children that they genuinely love them?

5. How might your local church benefit the community by being a good steward of God's resources?

CHAPTER 8: GIVING FOR THE RIGHT REASONS

1. What wrong motives accompanied Ananias and Sapphira's gift for the care of the needy?

2. How can emotional giving be poor stewardship?

3. What wrong motives for giving, cited by Dr. Bright, stood out to you and why? Have you known any fund-raising efforts that appealed to wrong motives? If so, how did they appeal to those motives?

4. If there were no tax exemptions for charitable giving, do you think such giving would decline or remain steady? Defend your answer.

5. If you received an unexpected $5,000 bonus, how would you allocate it?

CHAPTER 9: THE BLESSING OF THE TITHE

1. Why is it important to give according to a wise financial plan?

2. How can a Christian avoid tithing as a merely legalistic act?

3. How can tithing promote spiritual growth in the life of a tithing Christian?

4. Why do you agree or disagree that the New Testament teaches Christians to tithe?

5. What advice regarding tithing would you give to an unemployed head of a household?

CHAPTER 10: GOD WANTS YOU TO BE FINANCIALLY FREE

1. Why do you agree or disagree with the author's assertion that financial freedom "is available to every Christian steward

who faithfully follows God's plan for giving, saving, and spending"?

2. How do you define financial freedom?

3. How might financial freedom enable a believer to serve God better?

4. Why do so many Christians go so far into debt?

5. Do you agree or disagree that money can't buy happiness? Why?

CHAPTER 11: HOW TO BE FINANCIALLY FREE

1. What biblical principles should Christians apply when considering a big purchase?

2. How does the author describe "financial breathing"? How would this practice help you be a better steward?

3. What is the advantage of having a written financial plan?

4. How would you respond if a fellow Christian insisted that after giving a tithe to God he is free to spend the other 90 percent any way he wishes?

5. Why do you agree or disagree that a Christian should give 10 percent of his or her income to God, save 10 percent, and live on the remaining 80 percent?

CHAPTER 12: HOW TO TRUST GOD WITH YOUR FINANCES

1. How do you explain the fact that many wealthy people worry about finances?

2. Why is it better to trust in God than in money?

3. Why is God worthy of our trust? How has He shown His trustworthiness to you?

4. How can a Christian of meager income enjoy an abundant life?

5. What is the difference between a pledge and a faith promise?

CHAPTER 13: LIVE IT!

1. How has *The Joy of Dynamic Giving* been most helpful?

2. What key financial decisions do you believe every Christian should make? What decisions is God leading *you* to make as a result of reading this book?

3. How can giving to God's work be truly an adventure?

4. How can giving to God's work be a joyful experience?

5. Do you agree that the stewardship principles cited in this book apply equally to Christian millionaires and minimum-wage earners? Defend your answer.

Appendix

God's Word on Dynamic Giving

Following are selected Scripture references that were presented throughout the text of this book. We encourage you to sit down with your Bible and review these verses in their context, prayerfully reflecting upon what God's Word tells you about the joy of dynamic giving.

CHAPTER 1

Mark 16:15
John 10:10
3 John 1:2
Psalm 1:2–3
Psalm 24:1
Colossians 1:15–18
1 Peter 1:18–19
Ephesians 1:20–23
Matthew 25:14–30
Romans 14:12
Matthew 28:19

CHAPTER 2

2 Timothy 1:7
1 Corinthians 4:2
1 John 1:7
John 15:1–8
Luke 16:10–11
Acts 1:8

CHAPTER 3

Matthew 5:42
Matthew 10:8
Matthew 19:21
Luke 11:41
Matthew 25:33–40
Matthew 6:33
Colossians 3:2
1 Thessalonians
   5:18

Acts 20:35

CHAPTER 4

1 Chronicles
    29:11–12
Deuteronomy
    33:27
Jeremiah 23:24
Jeremiah 32:17
Romans 11:33–34
Exodus 15:11
John 14:6
Ephesians 2:4–5
Ephesians 5:15–16
1 Corinthians 12:7

CHAPTER 5

Philippians 4:19
Genesis 8:22
Luke 6:38
Genesis 22:17
Matthew 15:32
John 6:1–13
2 Corinthians
    9:6–10
Mark 1:32–34;
    3:10; 6:53–56
John 7:38
1 Corinthians
    15:58
James 2:14–18
2 Corinthians 8:9

Ephesians 2:6; 1:3
Colossians 1:28

CHAPTER 6

Genesis 1:11
Galatians 6:7–8
Hosea 10:12
Luke 19:12–27
John 12:25

CHAPTER 7

Luke 12:43
Matthew 22:37–40
Genesis 1:27–28
1 Timothy 5:8
Ephesians 5:25
Psalm 127:3
Psalm 103:13
Matthew 5:13–14
3 John 1:6
Galatians 6:10

CHAPTER 8

Acts 5:4
Romans 11:35
Acts 8:17–24
1 Timothy 6:6–7
2 Corinthians 5:9
Matthew 6:19–21

CHAPTER 9

1 Corinthians 16:2

Malachi 3:10
1 Chronicles 16:29
Psalm 29:2
Proverbs 3:9

CHAPTER 10

Philippians 4:11
Luke 12:42
1 Timothy 6:10
Proverbs 15:6
Ecclesiastes 5:19
Philippians 4:12
Luke 12:15
Proverbs 30:8–9
Mark 4:19
Ecclesiastes
    5:11–12
Proverbs 27:24
Matthew 6:19
1 Timothy 6:9

CHAPTER 11

Colossians 3:15
Romans 13:8

CHAPTER 12

Deuteronomy 8:18
Psalm 12:6
John 14:21
James 4:2
Jeremiah 33:3

About the Author

DR. BILL BRIGHT, fueled by his passion to share the love and claims of Jesus Christ with "every living person on earth," was the founder and president of Campus Crusade for Christ. The world's largest Christian ministry, Campus Crusade serves people in 191 countries through a staff of 26,000 full-time employees and more than 225,000 trained volunteers working in some sixty targeted ministries and projects that range from military ministry to inner-city ministry.

Bill Bright was so motivated by what is known as the Great Commission, Christ's command to carry the gospel throughout the world, that in 1956 he wrote a booklet titled *The Four Spiritual Laws*, which has been printed in 200 languages and distributed to more than 2.5 billion people. Other books Bright authored include *Discover the Book God Wrote, God: Discover His Character, Come Help Change Our World, The Holy Spirit: The Key to Supernatural Living, Life Without Equal, Witnessing Without Fear, Coming Revival, Journey Home,* and *Red Sky in the Morning.*

In 1979 Bright commissioned the *JESUS* film, a feature-length dramatization of the life of Christ. To date, the film has been viewed by more than 5.7 billion people in 191 countries and has become the most widely viewed and translated film in history.

Dr. Bright died in July 2003 before the final editing of this book. But he prayed that it would leave a legacy of his love for Jesus and the power of the Holy Spirit to change lives. He is survived by his wife, Vonette; their sons and daughters-in-law; and four grandchildren.

THE LIFETIME TEACHINGS OF

Written by one of Christianity's most respected and beloved teachers, this series is a must for every believer's library. Each of the books in the series focuses on a vital aspect of a meaningful life of faith: trusting God, accepting Christ, living a spirit-filled life, intimacy with God, forgiveness, prayer, obedience, supernatural thinking, giving, and sharing Christ with others.

Dr. Bill Bright was the founder of Campus Crusade for Christ Intl., the world's largest Christian ministry. He commissioned the JESUS film, a documentary on the life of Christ that has been translated into more than 800 languages.

EACH BOOK INCLUDES A CELEBRITY-READ ABRIDGED AUDIO CD!

 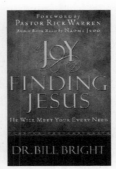 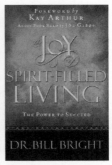

Joy of Trusting God
Foreword by Billy Graham
Audio by John Tesh
0-78144-246-X

Joy of Finding Jesus
Foreword by Pastor
Rick Warren
Audio by Naomi Judd
0-78144-247-8

Joy of Spirit-Filled Living
Foreword by Kay Arthur
Audio by Ricky Skaggs
0-78144-248-6

Dr. Bill Bright

FOUNDER OF CAMPUS CRUSADE FOR CHRIST

Joy of Supernatural Thinking
Foreword by John Maxwell
Audio by Gov. Mike Huckabee
0-78144-253-2

Joy of Dynamic Giving
Foreword by Charles Stanley
Audio by John Schneider
0-78144-254-0

Joy of Sharing Jesus
Foreword by Pat Robertson
Audio by Kathie Lee Gifford
0-78144-255-9

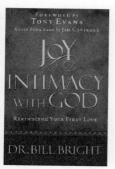

Joy of Intimacy with God
Foreword by Tony Evans
Audio by Amy Grant
0-78144-249-4

Joy of Total Forgiveness
Foreword by Gary Smalley
Audio by Janine Turner
0-78144-250-8

Joy of Active Prayer
Foreword by Max Lucado
Audio by Joni Earekcson Tada
0-78144-251-6

Joy of Faithful Obedience
Foreword by Tim LaHaye
Audio by Kirk Franklin
0-78144-252-4

Collect all 10 of These Foundational Works!

The Word at Work Around the World

A vital part of Cook Communications Ministries is our international outreach, Cook Communications Ministries International (CCMI). Your purchase of this book, and of other books and Christian-growth products from Cook, enables CCMI to provide Bibles and Christian literature to people in more than 150 languages in 65 countries.

Cook Communications Ministries is a not-for-profit, self-supporting organization. Revenues from sales of our books, Bible curricula, and other church and home products not only fund our U.S. ministry, but also fund our CCMI ministry around the world. One hundred percent of donations to CCMI go to our international literature programs.

CCMI reaches out internationally in three ways:

- Our premier International Christian Publishing Institute (ICPI) trains leaders from nationally led publishing houses around the world.

- We provide literature for pastors, evangelists, and Christian workers in their national language.

- We reach people at risk—refugees, AIDS victims, street children, and famine victims—with God's Word.

Word Power, God's Power

Faith Kidz, RiverOak, Honor, Life Journey, Victor, NexGen — every time you purchase a book produced by Cook Communications Ministries, you not only meet a vital personal need in your life or in the life of someone you love, but you're also a part of ministering to José in Colombia, Humberto in Chile, Gousa in India, or Lidiane in Brazil. You help make it possible for a pastor in China, a child in Peru, or a mother in West Africa to enjoy a life-changing book. And because you helped, children and adults around the world are learning God's Word and walking in his ways.

Thank you for your partnership in helping to disciple the world. May God bless you with the power of his Word in your life.

For more information about our international ministries, visit www.ccmi.org.

Additional copies of
THE JOY OF DYNAMIC GIVING
and other titles in "The Joy of Knowing God" series
are available wherever good books are sold.

✠ ✠ ✠

If you have enjoyed this book,
or if it has had an impact on your life,
we would like to hear from you.

Please contact us at:

VICTOR BOOKS
Cook Communications Ministries, Dept. 201
4050 Lee Vance View
Colorado Springs, CO 80918

Or at our Web site: www.cookministries.com

Victor®
The Bible Teacher's Teacher